# Shipwrecks
## of the Caribbean
### A Diver's Guide

Martha Watkins Gilkes

Interlink Books
An imprint of Interlink Publishing Group, Inc.
New York • Northampton

First American edition published 2003 by

**INTERLINK BOOKS**
An imprint of Interlink Publishing Group, Inc.
99 Seventh Avenue, Brooklyn, New York 11215 and
46 Crosby Street, Northampton, Massachusetts 01060
**www.interlinkbooks.com**

**Library of Congress Cataloging-in-Publication Data**
Gilkes, Martha Watkins.
Shipwrecks of the Caribbean: a diver's guide / by Martha Watkins Gilkes.
  p. cm.
ISBN 1–56656–476–X (pbk.)
1. Shipwrecks—Caribbean Sea. 2. Treasure-trove—Caribbean Sea. I. Title.
G525.G493 2002
910'.916365—dc21

                                                2002008861

Front cover engraving of the RMS *Rhone* by permission of Wavey Line
Publishing.
Front cover photograph of Martha Watkins Gilkes diving on the
*Rhone* by Armando Jenik. Back cover photograph of HMS Endymion
by *Robert Bulgin.*

The author and publishers would like to thank the following for
permission to reproduce their material: Charlotte Berglund; Steve
Birchall; Robert Bulgin; Richard McCrea; National Maritime Museum,
Greenwich; Lesley Runnalls; Wavey Line Publishing.
All other photographs are by Martha Watkins Gilkes.

To request our complete 40-page full-color catalog,
please call us toll-free at **1-800-238-LINK**, visit our
website at **www.interlinkbooks.com**, or write to:
Interlink Publishing, 46 Crosby Street, Northampton, MA 01060
e-mail: info@interlinkbooks.com

Colour separation by Tenon & Polert Colour Scanning Ltd

Printed and bound in Malaysia

2006  2005  2004  2003  2002
10  9  8  7  6  5  4  3  2  1

# Contents

I dedicate this book to Stan Waterman.

My first book, *Diving Guide to the Eastern Caribbean*, published in 1994, was dedicated to Stan. Now, nine years later, our twenty-year plus diving-oriented friendship has continued to flourish and provide new underwater adventures and experiences around the globe, including the exploration of shipwrecks. It was a shipwreck that brought us together in 1979: Stan was filming the story of the sinking of the *Stavronikita* off Barbados and I was diving on the site. Since that time we have explored many shipwrecks together, probably the most exciting being the massive Japanese warships of Turk Lagoon in the South Pacific (not covered in this guide). My hope and wish is that these exciting adventures continue for another twenty years!

# Acknowledgements

Soon after the publication of my first diving book, *Diving Guide to the Eastern Caribbean* (Macmillan), the seeds were sown for a sequel. Serious research on the shipwrecks of many of the remote and wonderful islands of the Eastern Caribbean had never been published in one book and the challenge to document and explore these underwater treasures was too exciting to ignore. My appetite for exploration of these wrecks had been whetted in the research for the first book.

This was shortly before the onslaught of one of the worst hurricanes of the century at that time: Hurricane Luis, in September 1995, literally blew me away. Without a safe haven, an office, or even a roof over my head, all dreams of writing a creative shipwreck book had 'gone with the wind'! In addition, the extensive research on shipwrecks which I had already undertaken for the publication of the first book was made useless by the onslaught of Hurricane Luis. Many of the shipwrecks noted in my first book were no longer visible; divable wrecks and many new wrecks were put down from the storm; the research had to begin again. After extensive delays and many excuses to my ever-patient publisher, I began island-hopping once again, diving and researching this exciting topic. Always in the back of my mind was the possibility of discovering an unknown treasure wreck; but equally or perhaps more exciting became the quest to unravel the mysteries behind many of the wrecks; often, even the long-time islanders had only sketchy information on the stories of these ladies of the deep.

When my research was well under way, in September 1998, Hurricane Georges struck the islands, causing much personal devastation to my life. However, once again I picked up the pieces and the research continued. In September 1999 I flew to London to turn over 98 per cent of my shipwreck research, returning to the islands in early October to complete the last 2 per cent. (Did my patient publisher really believe me?) On 19 October Hurricane Jose came barrelling over Antigua; before we could finish the clean-up Hurricane Lenny came charging towards Antigua *from the wrong direction* on 16 November. I was beginning to believe this shipwreck book was not meant to be finished!

I finally did get back to the grindstone and now this publication is the culmination of more years of work than I like to admit – because of the hurricanes that disrupted my life.

During my research, I became a detective, an investigator, a fact-finder, as I followed the trail from one fragment of information to another, trying to tie together the threads to tell the stories of these shipwrecks. Many of the facts on the wrecks cannot be documented. Often records do not exist, and many of those that did have been destroyed by hurricanes. Not all of the sites covered in this guide are regularly dived shipwrecks (sites to which the local island dive shops can and will take the tourist diver). On some islands I explore a combination of modern shipwrecks which are regularly dived on and also ancient shipwreck sites which may have been excavated. These sites have interesting stories but some are not divable as there is not enough remaining to be of great interest to tourist divers. Some research was done in London in *Lloyds Registry of Shipping* and other sources, but often the ships in the Caribbean waters were either not large enough to be mentioned or were not recorded for other reasons.

In some cases I met violent resistance to questions. On one island the owner of a significant shipwreck refused to talk to me. He claimed he had lost all he had when the ship sank; why should he talk with me on this unpleasant subject? For wreck divers, a wreck is an exciting adventure of exploration. For the owner who lost all in the sinking, there is another story, as I learned while researching this project.

I would also like to stress that the shipwrecks of these islands should be treated with respect by visiting divers. These wrecks provide historical documentation and should not be viewed as souvenir sites where the careless diver can try to pry out a porthole or brass nail or other such trinket to take home to place on the mantelpiece. Disturbing the shipwrecks can damage historical evidence, should the site later be excavated for archaeological purposes. In many of the islands there are now laws protecting the sites from such activity. As most of the dive shops tell visiting divers, take only pictures and leave only bubbles. If you do this, the sites can be enjoyed by divers in future years.

While I have endeavoured to be as accurate as possible, in many cases I have had to rely on word of mouth, interviews and discussions. I have tried to confirm and document the stories told to me, which I now share with my readers; it is my hope that the facts are all correct, but any corrections from readers would be greatly appreciated to PO Box

W 1924, Antigua, West Indies, or by email to gilkesm@candw.ag.

It would have been impossible for me to dive personally on every shipwreck covered, although I have travelled to every island mentioned and dived on and photographed at least some of the wrecks on each island. For the others I have relied on the details provided by seasoned dive operators on the islands; I have also obtained some photographs from various photographers. I greatly appreciate both sources of help.

It is very difficult to thank everyone who has helped in this enormous project but I have attempted to list, by island, those who kindly assisted me in this research. There are a few who have been especially instrumental in this venture and I would like to mention them specifically. If patience is really a virtue, the most virtuous person I know has to be Nicholas Gillard, the Caribbean editor for Macmillan. He 'inherited' me from his predecessor and was forced to suffer through my many excuses and delays (which ran to a few years!), refusing to allow me to wriggle out of this commitment! His encouragement to me was unrelenting. Stan Waterman, my mentor in diving of many years and my good friend, not only encouraged me in this project, but dived with me on a number of the wrecks covered in this text and kindly wrote the foreword for this second book. Edna Fortescue of F.T. Caribbean helped with the much-needed editing as well as continually encouraging me to get on with the job! Of course, my husband Tony cannot be left off the list of thank yous. Thanks to him for months (that became years) of patience while I went off chasing my dreams of underwater shipwrecks, instead of staying at home baking cookies (or even buying groceries)!

I would like to thank all the others who have helped in this endeavour. I hope that no one has been overlooked and if so, I offer sincere apologies.

## ANGUILLA
The Board of Tourism; The Dive Shop Anguilla Ltd, owner Thomas Peabody; David Carty; Dr David Berglund; Sir Emile Gumbs; Mr and Mrs Ian Smith of Spin Drift Apartments; Ian Smith of Anguilla National Trust.

## ANTIGUA AND BARBUDA
Desmond Nicholson of the Antigua and Barbuda Historical Society.

## BRITISH VIRGIN ISLANDS
BVI Tourist Board and National Parks; Muffy and Keith Royal of Blue Water Divers; Joe Giacinto of Dive BVI Ltd; Armando Jenik of Armando Jenik Underwater Productions.

## CAYMAN ISLANDS
Cayman Island Tourist Board; Dr Margaret E. Leshikar-Denton; Wayne Hasson of Aggressor Fleet; Barbara Currie Dailey.

## DOMINICA
Derek Perryman of Dive Dominica.

## GRENADA AND CARRIACOU
The Grenada Board of Tourism; HMC Watersports, owner Mosden Cumberbatch; Spice Divers Grenada Ltd, owner Peter Seupel; Andrew Bierzynski of the Grenada National Trust.

## ST KITTS AND NEVIS
The St Kitts and Nevis Board of Tourism; dive operators Nikki Sinibaldi of St Kitts Scuba and Kenneth Samuel of Kenneth's Dive Center; Al Barker; Jacklyn Armoney of St Kitts and Nevis Heritage Society.

## ST LUCIA
Alice Bagshaw.

## TURKS AND CAICOS
Bob Gascoine; Jane Minty; Dr Donald Keith; Bob Bulgin; Bill Musa.

## US VIRGIN ISLANDS
St Croix – Divemaster Ken Schull; Scuba West, owner Steve Garner; Scuba, owners Molly and Ed Buckley; Dive Experience, owner Michelle Pugh.

St Thomas – US Virgin Island Tourist Board; St Thomas Diving Club, owner Bill Letts; diver Kenneth Turbe; Captain Jim McManus of Sea Trade; Doug Spratte.

## ST VINCENT AND THE GRENADINES
Dive St Vincent, owner Bill Tewes.

## MISCELLANEOUS
The LIAT captains who helped get me there even during 'overcrowded flights, cancelled sectors, uncertain take-offs', especially: Captain John Murphy, Captain Gregory Deans, Captain Cameron, Captain Dewhurst, and Captain Alex Double of the UK for assistance in research.

Divers' Ambassador Tom Anderson, and Conner and Stan Huckaby for being my dive buddies on various wrecks.

Lee Snyder, Sean Heath and Yves Ephraim for computer expertise.

Photographers Lesley Runnalls, George Hume, Bob Erhard, Wayne Hasson and Richard McCrea for sharing their work.

# Foreword

I am not only pleased to write a foreword for Martha's new guide to wrecks of the Caribbean – I owe her one. She has been my regular, untiring and thoroughly professional dive buddy on scores of trips. More than once, when I was carried away by some animal behaviour scene I was shooting at one hundred or more feet, I got around to looking at my gauges and became alarmed too late to find I had 300 psi of air left and about a half hour of decompression ahead. That's when I started looking for Martha. She was always there, well above me, keeping an eye on her imprudent buddy, and ready to offer her octopus regulator with a good 1500 psi in reserve.

I am well aware of the calibre of Martha's work. On our diving trips I have watched her untiringly research her projects, busy with her lap top computer, the salon table piled with the references she is researching. Just as untiring are her travels through her familiar world of the Caribbean for on-location interviews with local divers and her photographic excursions to the actual wreck sites.

Few people know the Caribbean as well as Martha. Her *Diving Guide to the Eastern Caribbean*, successfully published and widely read by serious divers, was the product of exhaustive research. Her work for the US State Department has, over the years, taken her to every island in the far-reaching Caribbean chain. As the President (and progenitor) of the Caribbean Safe Diving Society she was the driving force behind the establishing of the first recompression chamber in her Caribbean neighbourhood (Barbados). Her home is on Antigua. She has taught legions of divers there, and honed her skills as a writer and underwater photographer. She is pre-eminently qualified for the authorship of this book.

Stan Waterman

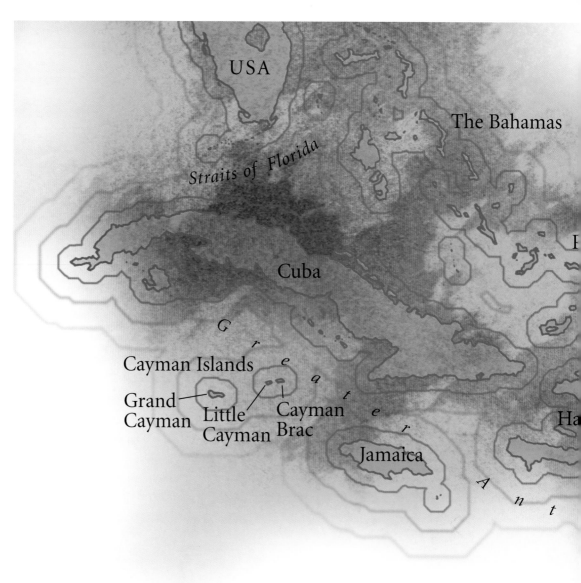

USA

The Bahamas

*Straits of Florida*

Cuba

Cayman Islands

*G r e a t e r*

Grand
Cayman

Little
Cayman

Cayman
Brac

Jamaica

*A n t*

Ha

*C A R I B B E A*

Colombia

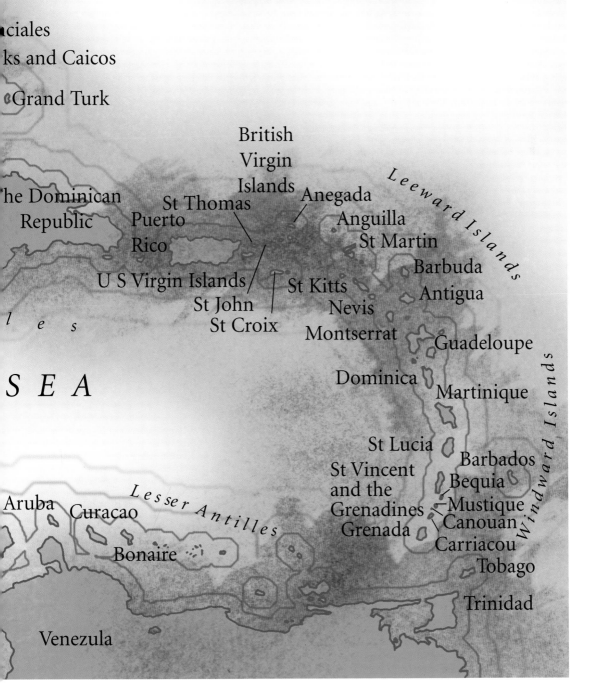

ATLANTIC OCEAN

ciales

ks and Caicos

Grand Turk

British
Virgin
Islands

Anegada

Leeward Islands

The Dominican
Republic

St Thomas

Anguilla

Puerto
Rico

St Martin

Barbuda

U S Virgin Islands

St Kitts

Antigua

St John

Nevis

les

St Croix

Montserrat

Guadeloupe

SEA

Dominica

Martinique

St Lucia

Barbados

St Vincent
and the
Grenadines

Bequia

Mustique

Lesser Antilles

Grenada

Canouan

Windward Islands

Aruba

Curaçao

Carriacou

Tobago

Bonaire

Trinidad

Venezula

# Introduction to Diving on Shipwrecks

Sunken ships, Spanish treasure, gold coins and medallions – all of these conjure up great excitement to scuba divers, who dream of stumbling upon an ancient shipwreck from days gone by! For divers, shipwrecks not only mean the possibility of finding interesting and valuable artefacts and unlocking a bit of history. They also mean a profusion of marine life. Wrecks attract a variety of sea creatures, which seek out nooks and crannies for shelter. In warm tropical waters marine growth also quickly attaches to wreck structures, forming an artificial reef on the seabed.

*(opposite)* **Martha Watkins and Stan Waterman on the** *Oro Verde* **off the waters of Grand Cayman**
*(Richard McCrea)*

**Martha Watkins Gilkes with a rare black coral tree**

The Caribbean is a paradise for wreck divers. There are wrecks scattered up and down the island chain and many of them have been there for centuries, sunk by hurricanes long ago. There are also a number of modern-day wrecks, intentionally sunk as scuba diving sites to attract divers and enhance the marine life. At the top of the list of the islands covered in this guide where shipwrecks have actively been placed as artificial reefs are Anguilla, Barbados, St Croix and St Lucia.

One of the most exciting and largest but also potentially dangerous shipwrecks for divers is the *Bianca C*, sunk off the south point of Grenada. This 584 ft lady will always be remembered throughout the island.

Barbados also claims a special shipwreck, the SS *Stavronikita*, a 356 ft Greek cargo ship intentionally sunk as a major scuba diving site. It was on this wreck site that I met Stan Waterman during an underwater film shoot in 1979. He was documenting the story of her sinking. Our twenty-year diving friendship has changed the course of my life, so the SS *Stavronikita* has a special place in my heart.

The British Virgin Islands are home to RMS *Rhone*, a 310 ft ocean steamer that sank during a hurricane in 1867. She is perhaps the most famous wreck of the Southern Caribbean, having gained her notoriety when she was chosen as the site for the filming of the Columbia Pictures film, *The Deep*, based on Peter Benchley's story of treasure diving. She has also been named the best wreck in the Caribbean by *Skin Diver* magazine.

St Vincent and the Grenadines have several wreck sites of interest, the most notable being the HMS *Purina*. This 140 ft World War I English gunboat lies just off Mayreau in only 40 ft of water. There is also a French warship in Kingstown harbour that is of great interest.

Wreck diving is a specialty and is not for the beginner diver. There are special considerations not needed in diving on a reef. Divers often become so absorbed in wreck exploration that they forget to monitor their gauges for time and depth limits. Many wreck divers are also underwater photographers, and this can distract one's attention from important safety procedures. Divers should be extremely careful when penetrating wrecks, as it is possible to become trapped; stirred up sediment can cause loss of visibility and hence obscure the exit route. Veteran diver Stan Waterman has a hair raising story to tell of a situation where the sediment deep within a World War II wreck nearly led to the end of his diving days! Sharp objects can be found inside wrecks, making them dangerous. Large marine life can take shelter inside a wreck, and while any threatening action would be from a defensive point, divers should be aware of sea creatures that may be in the wreck. However, as is the case in all diving, proper training is the key. Divers seriously interested in wreck exploration should undertake a certification course in this area. I have become a wreck diving fanatic during this project so would never discourage divers from enjoying an exciting aspect of our sport. I hope that I will be able to open up the world of wreck diving to many of my diving fraternity buddies.

**Martha Watkins Gilkes**
**photographing underwater**

# Unusual Marine Encounters

**George the barracuda with Stan Waterman on the wreck of the *Stavronikita* in Barbados**
*(Lesley Runnalls)*

Divers fascinated by the marine environment dream of diving with special creatures of the sea. We travel far and wide seeking encounters with unusual marine creatures.

In thirty years of diving and over 8000 dives I have encountered an array of marine creatures. Many of these animals have been associated with shipwrecks; wrecks are known to attract marine life. Some of my encounters are especially memorable and include Honey, the wild dolphin who lives off the clear waters of Lighthouse Reef near Belize, Buddha the barracuda whose home is Tent Reef off Saba, and his cousin, George, who lived inside the wreck of the *Stavronikita* in Barbados. I have dived with the friendly stingrays of the famous Stingray City in the Cayman Islands and have had encounters with large schools of hammerhead sharks off Costa Rica. I have had manta encounters with the mantas of Yap and with the very special Molly the manta who lived for several years in Little Cayman.

Perhaps the most bizarre behaviour I have witnessed was that of George the barracuda. George took up residence on the big wreck of the *Stavronikita* lying in the waters off Barbados and for several years was nearly always to be found there. He would hang vertically in a companionway in the great ship as he admired his reflection in a large air bubble trapped on the ceiling. The 'mirror' was formed from the exhaled compressed air of divers swimming through. There was speculation on why a fish would behave this way: some felt he thought the reflection was another barracuda; others said he was narcissistic and was in love with his own image. For whatever reason, the behaviour provided close encounters and wonderful photo opportunities for divers. The photographer could approach from one entrance while another diver entered from a second doorway; this created a great set-up of George in the foreground with the diver behind. George never posed any threat to divers, contrary to the belief that barracudas are vicious!

Buddha the barracuda from Saba was another 'friendly' photo subject. Buddha lived under the massive overhangs of Tent Reef. He learned that when divers fed the smaller conies and reef fish, as was

once the custom to attract fish life, he could easily sneak a nibble from an unsuspecting fish interested in the free handout of food. Buddha would allow divers to close in on both sides, setting the stage for a great photo under the coral overhangs. He was another 'dangerous marine creature' who proved that the barracuda is not so threatening after all.

The waters off Dominica offer a most unique dive site, which also attracts squid. Divers often sight squid on dives but here it is an unusual experience.

There is a marine subaquatic hot freshwater spring, not found on many other islands, just offshore in only 10–20 ft of water, known as 'Champagne'. Freshwater bubbles drift slowly through holes and cracks in the rock formation towards the surface, appearing like liquid crystal glistening in the sunlight, or perhaps champagne bubbles rising in a glass. This is the perfect ending to a night dive as one ascends from the nearby reef to the hot bubbles, and experiences nature's sauna. On almost every night dive at 'Champagne' divers are greeted by schools of squid, adding to the already exotic atmosphere. On this dive the squid seem to be mesmerised by a combination of the warm bubbles and the divers' underwater lights and have allowed divers to stroke them.

Buddha the barracuda on Tent Reef in Saba with diver Barbara Currie Dailey

Diver Lucy Stickney on a night dive with squid, which have been attracted by the underwater light

Belize is home to Oscar, a massive friendly grouper. I encountered Oscar on several trips to dive the waters of Belize. For some years Oscar was fed and this was the initial attraction for divers. He became 'tame' and would approach every time divers entered the water. The first time I spotted him I was unaware of his friendly nature and was somewhat taken aback by his aggressive approach. However, he only wanted a handout. Oscar set the stage for many great underwater photographs and will be remembered by all divers who encountered him in the Belize waters.

Stingray City off Grand Cayman has been dubbed the world's greatest 12 ft dive. It has certainly provided many divers with amazing encounters with massive stingrays. Stingray City is located in Grand Cayman's North Sound, and can be reached only by boat. Actually this attraction is old news to local fishermen and boat captains. Stingrays have frequented the area for decades. Veteran North Sound captain 79-year-old Captain Marvin Ebanks says he remembers rays congregating there as far back as the 1930s. It was a popular calm, shallow anchorage where boats could clean their catches before returning to shore. Leftover bait and fish parts attracted the rays, who found a free lunch year round.

*(previous spread)*
**Martha Watkins Gilkes introducing Oscar to divers Bona Macy and Barbara Athill**

**Martha Watkins Gilkes at Stingray City in Grand Cayman**

The site was 'discovered' in a different way in summer 1986 when local divemasters Pat Kinney and Jay Ireland noticed that the gathering of rays seemed to allow human interaction. They began to work with the animals, attempting to feed them by hand. The rest is history. Nearby, the shallower Sand Bar has also become a favourite snorkelling spot, visited by hundreds each week. The rays gather here, in less than 4 ft of water, greeting snorkellers and swimmers – and obviously expecting food in return.

The unusual behaviour of the rays has fascinated marine biologists, who so far have not been able to present a scientific explanation for the creatures' affinity for human company other than the obvious one – easy food all day long.

During the last 11 years, Stingray City has been featured in international publications including *National Geographic* and highlighted in many films. Stingray City and Sand Bar offer both divers and snorkellers a thrilling experience, which has been safely enjoyed by thousands of visitors each year. The experience has changed the way many view stingrays!

Moray eels are considered by many as particularly vicious. Over the years there have been a number of moray eels that have been 'tamed' by patient divemasters and instructors. I have experienced several encounters with 'friendly' moray eels.

In Antigua Mitilda, a massive 5½ ft green moray, lived in the waters near Sunken Rock, an exciting dive site on the Atlantic side of the island.

**Diver John Charlesworth in Antigua with Mitilda the friendly green moray eel**

Iain Grumitt, former
part-owner of Tamarian
Watersports in Anguilla,
greeting his pet black
spotted moray eel on the
wreck of the MV *Ida
Maria*; diver Tony Gilkes
looks on

Owner of Aquanaut Divers John Charlesworth befriended her in the summer of 1996, initially at a dive site called Eric's Gardens, so named because the reef is directly under the home of rock star Eric Clapton. John began to offer her handouts of fish when he was on the dive site, perhaps once a week. One day she appeared at nearby Sunken Rock, where John dived almost daily. He began feeding her at this location. Over time she became so friendly she would swim between his legs seeking out her free lunch. The rapport continued for 18 months, when she disappeared. She returned after four months, just as friendly. She never once bit or injured any of the divers during her feedings. She remained for another six months when, once again, she disappeared. Sadly she has never returned. During her time I dived several times with her and enjoyed the unique experience of watching the interaction she allowed between diver and moray.

In Anguilla wreck diving is strongly promoted. The government has intentionally sunk a number of large wrecks. The 110 ft *Ida Maria* was sunk in 1984. She soon became home to a number of marine animals including a black spotted moray eel. Dive shop owners Iain Grumitt and Thomas Peabody began hand feeding the eel and befriended it. I first dived this site in the late eighties and witnessed and photographed Iain actually tickling the moray under the chin! For many years the eel was hand fed and was always seen on the wreck. After Hurricane Hugo in 1989, Iain and Thomas noticed the eel was badly damaged and literally had his skull split open. Sadly, they noticed his continued decline, until the friendly eel was no longer seen. However, for a number of years this friendly eel delighted divers as they watched the rapport between diver and eel.

Rarely will a large marine creature interact with a diver. The moment lives on for ever in the minds of those who have such an underwater experience. Molly the manta has been featured on the cover of one of the tourist publications for the Cayman Islands. She is one of the most photographed marine creatures in the waters around the Islands.

Molly first appeared in the waters of Cayman around March 1991, according to J.D. Sailer, divemaster at Reef Divers. Her encounters with the live-aboard dive boats were on a daily basis and she joined the divers on most night dives. The strong underwater lights would attract plankton, which Molly fed on. As divers sat on a sandy bottom with lights pointed into mid-water, Molly would appear out of the blackness and do barrel rolls in front of the divers' lights as she opened her gills to filter feed on the plankton. Her home was Jackson Bight Reef, off the island of Little Cayman, although she cruised up and down the reef wall as far north as Bloody Bay Point and as far south as Cayman Brac.

Molly had at least two close encounters with disaster. In the autumn of 1993 she became dangerously entangled in a turtle net but was able to return to the anchorage of the dive boats, where divers carefully freed her from the net. Without this rescue she would have died. In 1994 she appeared with a large fish hook piercing her lip and heavy line trailing. Again, according to Sailer, she approached divers, lay on the bottom and allowed them to remove the hook.

Molly the manta, who lived off **Cayman Brac** for some years, befriends divers on a night dive as she feeds off plankton
*(Bobby Erhard)*

Although Molly was a completely wild manta, for some years she chose the company of divers on a regular basis. An encounter with her was a 'magical moment with magnificent Molly' and one I will not forget.

Unfortunately, Molly is no more. Some think she may have been mistreated by careless divers. According to Wayne Hasson of the *Aggressor* fleet, in November 1995 he had just been on a night dive with environmental film maker Jean Michel Cousteau and Caymanian Minister of Tourism Thomas Jefferson. They observed divers from a live-aboard entering the water and chasing Molly, attempting to grab her. This resulted in Molly being declared a National Treasure of the Cayman Islands and the dive shops adopted a No Touch rule. But Molly soon disappeared and no longer interacts with divers. Hasson also commented that his boat captains, who knew Molly well, later saw her at least three times in the nearby waters but she did not approach divers. It is hoped that a lesson was learned by all about the abuse of marine animals.

I have also encountered the wonderful mantas of Yap Island in the Pacific. Here, inside a sheltered large lagoon in Mi'l Channel, 10–14 ft massive mantas congregate to be cleaned by cleaning wrasse in a special area. The cleaning stations are coral formations elevated from the channel bottom in 30–60 ft. Small wrasse and other fish specialise in grooming the mantas, nibbling away at parasites in the gills and on the skin, getting a free meal while the manta is rid of the parasite. Yap Divers discovered this some years ago and now they take divers to witness this amazing phenomenon, being careful not to interfere or disturb the mantas. Like my experience of watching Molly feeding and interacting with the divers in Cayman, this was a unique scene to witness.

Dolphins are irresistible, drawing people to them naturally with their eternal smiles. Most people only see photographs of them or perhaps observe them performing in captivity in a marine park. Some, like myself, are fortunate enough to enter the dolphin's world briefly and share a unique interaction between two mammals.

Honey is a wild Atlantic bottlenose dolphin who for some years has befriended boaters, swimmers and divers in the shallow, warm waters about 50 miles off Belize. I was lucky enough to enjoy spending several hours in the water with her as she played, frolicked and cavorted all around me.

No one knows where Honey came from or why she has left her pod and sought out human company, but she has now made her home inside a protected reef of Lighthouse Reef, greeting any boat that comes into the bay. She is delighted with the interaction of humans; so much so that when I attempted to exit the ladder she interceded, trying to prevent me from leaving her world.

**Martha Watkins Gilkes with fresh lobsters, still readily available on many remote islands**

This experience was shared with underwater film maker Stan Waterman, who has spent a lifetime filming marine animals, especially sharks. When asked his feeling on the experience, he commented: 'The privilege of having a wild dolphin accept you is one of the finest experiences one can have in the marine environment. It is a magic moment. You hear very seldom about such an encounter.'

Indeed, while there are several locations around the world that sponsor dolphin encounters, most of these are with captive dolphins.

The numbers of wild dolphins who have chosen interaction with human company are certainly limited; they include a few well-known ones like Jojo, who has been made a National Treasure in the Turks and Caicos Islands, and Donald, who was known in the waters of the UK some years ago.

The experience left me touched and feeling very fortunate that I had been part of a reaching out and acceptance between two totally different animals and that I could commune and share this unique time with one of the most intelligent of the marine mammals.

These encounters are some of the more personal ones with specific marine creatures. There have been other magical moments of being surrounded by large schools of pelagic creatures, where nature is truly master. It is occasions like these that keep divers seeking that unique experience below the waves.

Honey the wild dolphin, who lives in the waters off Lighthouse Reef, Belize

# Anguilla

Anguilla, along with St Croix, has more interesting, divable shipwrecks than any other Eastern Caribbean island covered in this guide. Of the wrecks covered here, eight are particularly suitable for diving, with structure to explore. Local experts have taken very seriously the knowledge that wreck diving is appealing more and more to sport divers. The choice of wrecks is so varied that for an avid wreck diver, the problem is deciding which wrecks to dive and explore! Anguilla is the only island covered here to have a book devoted to its wrecks – *Shipwrecks of Anguilla 1628–1993*, by Dr David Berglund. He has kindly shared his information and research with me and has consented to the use of his facts in this text. His book is a more comprehensive list of all Anguilla wrecks than can be covered in one chapter. For those interested, copies can be obtained direct from him at PO Box 130, Anguilla, BWI.

The earliest recorded wreck around Anguillan waters, according to Robert Marx's *New World Shipwrecks 1492–1825*, was a Spanish merchantman sailing from Puerto Rico to Spain. She was wrecked on the northern shore of the island on 12 December 1628. Frenchmen from nearby St Kitts salvaged most of the cargo, according to Marx.

For the most part these ancient wrecks, although recorded, have not been located. There was a discovery, however, of two interesting ancient Spanish wrecks that went down in 1772. The 990 ton *El Buen Consejo* ('The Good Consular'), an official government ship, was a frigate. She carried 70 guns. Along with the 673 ton *Jesu, Maria y Jose* (a 40 gun armed merchant vessel) she was wrecked on the southeast of the island. It is a mystery why these ships were in this area. According to Dr David Berglund, twice a year fleets sailed from Spain to the New World colonies. Because the islands in the Lesser Antilles had become populated with ever-increasing numbers of non-Spanish colonials (who often warred with Spain) the Spanish had to alter the pattern of the sailing routes used by the flotas. In this case, the flota had not put into port for any reprovisioning because of extreme danger of attack. It was making for landfall at St Bartholomew, and after sighting this, passed Anguilla to the north, headed for Anegada. Once it had cleared Anegada, the flota continued on a westerly course, passing north of Puerto Rico. Why these two ships became separated from the others is still a major question. These sites have been the centre of some controversy in salvage and are not open to sport divers. In addition the conditions on the rough Atlantic side of the island are not favourable to safe diving.

The effort and interest in deliberately sinking shipwrecks started in 1985. It was the brainchild of the owners of the pioneer dive shop on the island, Tamarian Watersports (now renamed The Dive Shop Anguilla Ltd), then owned by Thomas Peabody and Iain Grumitt. The MV *Ida Maria* was the first ship sunk that year, followed by the MV *Commerce* the next year. In 1990 four major ships were sunk and in 1993 the most recent wreck was put down. At present there are two more likely candidates washed ashore in Road Bay which may add to the list of divable wrecks!

In the summer of 1990 the government of Anguilla formed a marine task force, under the Ministry of the Environment. The parliamentary secretary and Minister of Education and the Environment, Mr David Carty, spearheaded the task force, along with four other volunteers. On 7 November 1984, during Hurricane Klaus, four large cargo ships were sunk or grounded inside Sandy Ground harbour. They were not only an eyesore, but were blocking the harbour. Carty felt strongly about this environmental problem and the need to clean it up, so action was taken. He enlisted the help of the Resolve Salvage Company, based in Fort Lauderdale, Florida. Between June and July 1990 the company sank four major shipwrecks: the MV *Oosterdiep* on 15 June, the MV *Meppel* and the MV *Lady Vie* on 28 June and finally the MV *Sarah* on 29 June. The MV *Christobel* was another major wreck salvaged by Resolve. She was sold to help pay the salvage operation costs.

**The wreck of the *Sarah* as she lay in Sandy Ground harbour**

The MV **Sarah**, a freighter, the largest of the ships sunk, is 222 ft long. She was 37 ft wide and had a draft of 13 ft. Her final sinking in 1990 drew the attention of the entire population of Anguilla, and a flotilla of all types of boats accompanied her to her final resting place to witness her disappearance beneath the waves.

The MV *Sarah* was constructed by the Grangemouth Dockyard Company Ltd on the Firth of Forth on the east coast of Scotland. She was completed on 9 March 1956 and began her life as the *Gannet*, a general purpose, dry cargo vessel. She was renamed *Sarah* by her second owner, in honour of his mother, and moved to Newfoundland. In 1983 she was moved to the Caribbean when the Anguilla Marine Transportation Company Ltd purchased her. She was often used to transport cement from Cuba to Anguilla and also carried animal feed. In fact, she went down with animal feed onboard; some feed that had been trapped in air pockets remained when she was refloated six years later.

On 7 November 1984 the MV *Sarah* was at her usual anchorage in Sandy Ground Bay. Hurricane Klaus unexpectedly hit Anguilla. It was Election Day in the USA and it is said that the weather satellite was not functioning properly. As people in the USA were so absorbed in the elections, the satellite was not repaired and thus Anguillans were unaware of the approaching hurricane; had they known, there would not have been so many marine-related losses. East of the anchorage of MV *Sarah* lay the remains of the *Ekco*, a small merchant ship that had sunk in the early spring of 1984 during rough weather. She lay just below the waterline and when the wind from Hurricane Klaus unexpectedly blew from the west, the MV *Sarah* swung on her anchor, hitting the *Ekco*, which then put two small holes in the hull of the *Sarah*. She took on water and settled to the bottom, lying above the waterline on her starboard side. For nearly six years she lay in the centre of the harbour. On 27 June 1990 she was pulled upright and refloated. This was a challenging operation even for a big commercial salvage company. First, three large derricks were welded onto the port side of *Sarah*. Airbags were then attached to her starboard side, beneath the water. A sand channel was dredged alongside her hull to allow her to be pulled upright. As the airbags were filled, cables attached to the derricks were tightened by two large tugs. After some five hours, the MV *Sarah* was pulled upright and was once again afloat. The two holes on her

**The wreck of the *Sarah***

**The wreck of the
*Commerce***

starboard side which had caused her sinking were temporarily patched and the large derricks on her port side helped balance her. She lay at anchor for two more days; at 1.15 p.m. on 29 June she was towed out of the harbour to the eastern end of the Sail Reef system by the same two tugs that had lifted her, accompanied by a large number of onlookers. Once she was in place, two of the three derricks were removed from her hull for future use. The third remains attached to her today. Finally at 4.30 pm, the temporary patches covering the holes that had sunk her were removed; she filled with water and disappeared beneath the waves.

She now rests totally intact and upright in 80 ft of water, with the shallowest part in 30 ft. Common marine life around her includes rays, barracudas and schools of jacks. The superstructure, left intact, makes an excellent backdrop for underwater photography. There are two large cargo holds in the stern section and two in the bow section. Divers can swim from one hold to the other in the bow section.

The MV **Commerce**, a 137 ft freighter built in Holland in 1955, lies in 45–80 ft of water off Flat Cap Point. She was 24 ft wide and had a gross tonnage of 143 tons. She originally worked as a general cargo ship on European trade routes for some 21 years. She was then purchased by Mr Clement Daniels, who used her as a cargo ship throughout the islands. In 1986, having been donated by her owner, she was the second large cargo ship intentionally sunk as a dive site, again through the organisational efforts of Peabody and Grumitt. She was a derelict boat anchored in Sandy Ground harbour, her engines unworkable, before being towed to her final resting place by the police boat and anchored in the chosen location. Her seacocks were opened and after about an hour of taking on water she sank to the bottom.

She sits upright on a sloping bottom, but when she went down she settled broadside and her centre section has been torn apart by the seas and is a jumble of metal, although the bow and stern are intact. Her propeller is also still there, half buried by sand. The structure is very open and allows divers to swim through her in complete safety. As she has been down for some years there is a large variety of fish life on the wreck – schools of Atlantic spadefish, barracuda, grunts and schooling jacks can usually be seen. Occasionally large stingrays have been spotted!

The MV **Ida Maria**, a 110 ft freighter, built at the time of World War I in the United Kingdom (possibly on the Clyde), was also intentionally sunk in 1985. She sits upright, semi-intact, in 60 ft of water. She

**MV** *Sarah*, awaiting removal by the salvage company; three large derricks are welded to her port side

A friendly barracuda
on the wreck
of the *Commerce*

started her life as a general cargo vessel on European trade routes, mostly in the Baltic countries, until she was sold and brought to the Caribbean by Mr Freddie Hughes in 1977. He used her to transport cargo from Trinidad to Puerto Rico and the islands in between. In November 1984 Hurricane Klaus was responsible for her sinking, along with that of several other ships. A tragic result of her demise was the damage she did to the *Warspite* as she dragged her anchor. This caused the ultimate sinking of the most loved of the old time wooden vessels of Anguilla; nearly all of Anguilla is said to have grieved when it became evident after the hurricane that the *Warspite* had been sunk. The story of the *Warspite* is told at the end of this chapter.

Although the MV *Ida Maria* was still afloat after the hurricane she was badly damaged, so her owner donated her to be sunk as a diving attraction. Penetration of this wreck is not allowed, as it is not safe.

The propeller
of the *Commerce*

The site affords the diver a unique interaction with marine life as the divemasters have hand fed the marine creatures at the wreck and they are most approachable! I first dived this site in the late eighties. At that time Iain Grumitt and Thomas Peabody had been hand feeding a black spotted moray eel, and for many years it was always spotted on the wreck. Other marine life includes large French angelfish, schools of Atlantic spadefish, rock beauties and exceptionally large spotted drums. Lobsters have also made this site home. This is a splendid site for abundant marine life and good photographic material.

The wreck of the MV *Oosterdiep*, sunk as part of the 1990 summer sinking programme, lies in 75 ft of water off Barnes Bay. She is intact and sits upright. Owned by Harry Franklin and used as a general cargo ship between the islands, she broke anchor on a perfectly calm day and was washed ashore in Sandy Ground. The remains of a car lie inside the cargo hold and another is outside the wreck, with the seats still recognisable. She is considered one of the best diving wrecks by the dive shops as she attracts schools of horse-eye cavaliers and jacks and other interesting marine life.

The *Oosterdiep*

The *Cathely H* covered in rich marine growth

The MV *Meppel*, also owned by Harry Franklin, was the third vessel sunk during 1990, in 80 ft of water. Like the MV *Oosterdiep*, she was washed up on the beach at the end of Sandy Ground. She is intact and sits upright on a sandy bottom just inside Sail Reef system, in the northeast corner.

The MV *Lady Vie*, the last of the four ships sunk in 1990, also lies in 80 ft, upright and intact not far from the Sail Reef system. Marine life includes turtles, spadefish, angelfish, stingrays and grunt.

*Cathely H*, 130 ft long, is the most recently sunk ship. She was originally owned by Kenneth Harrigan and was used as a general cargo ship between Anguilla, San Juan, British Virgin Islands and St Thomas. Thomas Peabody, who now dives regularly on her, recalls sailing on her several times in her prior life as a working cargo ship. After sitting at anchor in the harbour for several years, she was considered a shipping hazard and was sunk in November 1993 in 60 ft on a sandy bottom off Sandy Ground.

The *Marva W* lies in deep water at 140–80 ft; she is not dived by the dive shops owing to her depth but is worth mentioning. According to those who have dived on her, she attracts large marine life. She belonged to the family of Sir Emile Gumbs, former prime minister of Anguilla.

The *Warspite*, mentioned earlier and tragically lost during Hurricane Klaus, is still remembered with affection by most of Anguilla. The Gumbs family were her owners, and Sir Emile Gumbs kindly consented to an interview, to tell me the history of this noble ship. Sir Emile served as the captain of the *Warspite* from 1955 until 1963. When asked what her main cargo was, he laughingly commented that she carried anything, anytime, if the price was right! Although nothing remains of her for divers to explore or dive on, a chapter on the shipwrecks of Anguilla would not be complete without her story. She was the last remaining wooden schooner of the once proud fleet that ploughed the waters between Anguilla and the Dominican Republic, often taking the men of Anguilla to cut the sugar cane. She was also well known as far afield as the coast of Venezuela, and even in the ABC islands of Aruba, Bonaire and Curacao. In the early 1900s Anguilla was well known for its shipwrights and their skill in wooden boatbuilding. The *Gazelle*, as the *Warspite* was originally called, was built in 1909 in Anguilla, as a sailing sloop. In 1916 Mr Arthur Carty altered her bow section by adding some 11 ft. She took part in World

War I and it seemed appropriate that she should be renamed the *Warspite*. For some years she transported over one hundred men back and forth to the Dominican Republic. Because the decks were overcrowded the decision was made in 1929 to extend her length again. She was beached in Anguilla and cut in two, with 14 ft added to her mid-section; this time when launched she was a proud 75 ft, drawing 9 ft and carrying 75 tons of cargo.

There are many stories about the *Warspite*. She was nearly sunk off the Grenadines, and converted from windpower to optional auxiliary power; her captain once remarked that she was so fast that she skipped from the top of one wave to the top of the next without using the trough. Douglas C. Pyle also prominently features the *Warspite* in his book *Clean Sweet Wind: Sailing Craft of the Lesser Antilles*. After Hurricane Klaus, the broken remains of the *Warspite* were recovered and stored. The Anguilla Archaeological and Historical Society is committed to creating a memorial to the *Warspite*, possibly a large-scale model and a museum display. Divers visiting Anguilla who appreciate the old classic ships should check with the society on the latest status of this project. You might be lucky enough to see a model of this beautiful lady of the wind (and if you are especially fortunate, you might be privy to a conversation with Sir Emile or others who knew her, and hear some of her exciting sailing stories).

There are so many choices of exciting wreck sites in Anguilla that it is difficult to decide which ones to dive. Perhaps for an ideal diving holiday you should plan enough time to dive on all of them!

# Antigua and Barbuda

**Antigua:**
1. *Andes*
2. *Harbor of St John's*
3. *Unknown Barge*
4. *Warrior Geraint*
5. *Jetias*
6. HMS *Weymouth*
7. *Lady Caroline*
8. *Erna*
9. *Rickett Bottle Wreck*

**Barbuda:**
10. Spanish Ship – possibly 1695 *Santiago de Cullerin*
11. HMS *Griffin*
12  *Red Jacket*
13. SS *Croyden*
14. SS *Polrose*
15. SS *Amersfoort*

The underwater terrain of Antigua tends to match the land above. Antigua is a coral island; this makes the majority of the island very flat. It is said that there are 1000 square miles of coral reef surrounding the twin island states of Antigua and Barbuda. And where there are coral reefs, there are shipwrecks!

Compared to some of the Caribbean islands where ships have been intentionally sunk as diving attractions, Antigua and Barbuda are not particularly known as wreck diving islands. In fact, some of the dive operators do not like to encourage wreck diving as they feel the sites are disappointing when compared to living coral reefs.

However, there are records of many wrecks, and these have been collected for a book on Antigua shipwrecks by local historian Desmond Nicholson, of the Antigua Archaeological and Historical Society. He notes over 149 shipwrecks from 1572 to the present, the earliest being a Spanish sloop. Many of the wrecks have never been located or are so old they are difficult for the average diver to recognise underwater. For more information on Mr Nicholson's book, enquire at the Museum of Antigua and Barbuda.

Barbuda, like Antigua a very flat island and surrounded by treacherous coral reefs, is also known to have seen the ending of many ships of days gone by; it was the site of a major salvage operation by Mel Fisher (of the *Atocha* shipwreck fame). Robert Marx, author of *New World Shipwrecks* refers to some 28 wrecks around Antigua between 1666 and 1823, and notes 24 around Barbuda between 1695 and 1822.

## Antigua

There are a few modern day wrecks around Antigua, which are occasionally dived by the local diving shops. Some of the wrecks are badly broken up and can be disappointing if one is expecting an intact shipwreck. However, some of the sites can be interesting dives for the enthusiast.

Among the more modern wrecks is the **Andes**, a cargo ship, now lying in Deep Bay in only 19–20 ft of water; the shallow depth also makes this a good site for snorkelling. She sank on 9 June 1905 after catching fire the previous day in the harbour in St John's. She was carrying 1330 barrels of pitch from Trinidad to Valparaiso, presumably from Trinidad's pitch lake. Osbourne, Graham and Company of Sunderland built the *Andes*, a sailing vessel, in 1874. Her gross tonnage was 866 tons, her length was 207 ft, her beam 33½ ft and her depth 19½ ft. Her original port of registration was Hull, England and her owners were Channel Dry Docks, S.B. & E. Co. Captain R. Griffiths was her captain.

First onboard after the fire broke out was the harbourmaster and receiver of wrecks, Mr Walter Thompson, along with Lloyds representative Mr R. W. Dobson. After a survey was done, the harbourmaster had her moved to Deep Bay to avoid obstructing the harbour. The Lloyds representative promptly sent a cable to the London owners with a recommendation from the surveyor that the cargo be discharged. In a second telegram sent to the salvage association on 10 June, it was

*(opposite)*
**Nelson's dockyard in English Harbour, home base for Lord Nelson's warships**

stated that the *Andes* had been totally destroyed by fire and that only 180 barrels of the cargo had been saved. The hull was lying in 19 ft of water in Deep Bay.

As a final chapter in the life of the *Andes*, there were two more cables sent from the Lloyds agent on 27 and 29 June. The first recommended prompt sale of salvaged cargo by auction and the salvor claimed 75 per cent as arranged with the captain. The last telegram noted that the salvor had possession of everything and delivery was refused unless the terms offered were acceptable. It was confirmed that the hull had no value. As this was the last official mention in the Lloyds listings of the *Andes*, it would appear that the owners gave up and left everything to the salvors. Today, except for the little information noted in the Lloyds listing, the site in Deep Bay is the only testament to the *Andes*.

Just outside Deep Bay, on the south side of the entrance to St John's Harbour, where she came to her final resting place in 40 ft of water, is the ***Harbor of St John's***. She was a 90 ft steel tug and sank in 1967 in St John's Harbour while the water pump was being repaired. The water pump and 6 ft bronze propeller can still be seen.

About 60 ft behind the *Harbor of St John's* and 20 ft to the left one can find the remains of an old barge, known locally as the **Unknown Barge**. She was owned by Devcon but was badly leaking. For some time she was used by day as a barge, then pulled into the mud flats at night where she would sink into the mud, to be pumped out the following day. Dive Antigua, the longest established dive shop on the island, sank her in 1990. She now provides a home for schools of small reef fish!

Just off Maiden Island, the **Warrior Geraint** sank on 21 February 1972, at 12.36 p.m. while on a day cruising tour. A gas explosion caused the fire. All passengers were safely put ashore, but the owner and captain, Mr Anthony A. Garton, was badly burned. The *Warrior Geraint* was an ex-submarine chaser ML281 converted to a passenger vessel. She was built by the Diesel Construction Company on the Thames and was 112 ft long with an 18 ft beam. She carried two 671 GM diesel engines which remain. However, little else now remains of the wreck to attest to her existence.

Probably the most frequently dived wreck site in Antigua is off Diamond Bank. The 300 ft British steamship **Jetias** sank around 1917 as she was departing for the UK. She lies in shallow water (about 25 ft). She had a triple expansion steam engine with three cylinders, connecting rods, control rods, condenser and two boilers, which are still intact after sinking. She also retains her four-blade prop, which makes a good setting for underwater photographs.

HMS **Weymouth**, an English warship, for which the reef off Sandy Island is named, went aground on 16 February 1745. She was built at Plymouth dockyard and launched on 3 March 1736. She was 144 ft long and her beam was 41½ ft. Her 60 gun armaments included 26 24-pounders, 26 12-pounders and eight 6-pounders. There was a court martial held for Captain Warwick Calmady, who was acquitted, but Lt Crispe 'forfeited six months' pay and  was declared incapable of serving'. The pilot was imprisoned in Jamaica. The scattered remains of the ship are heavily encrusted, but lie among the reef as reminders of her sad ending.

There are three or four other wrecks around Weymouth Reef and Sandy Island and anchors and cannon can be spotted in various locations!

On the Atlantic side of Antigua one wreck has become known as the **Lady Caroline** after the daughter of the dive shop owner responsible for sinking her. The vessel was damaged by Hurricane Luis, which ravaged

Peter Benchley exploring
the *Rickett Bottle Wreck*

Antigua for 36 hours in September 1995, and because of subsequent additional damage she is no longer considered worth diving on. She lies in 100 ft of water just over a coral drop-off directly off Mamora Bay, location of the St James Club. Although the mast is gone, she still has her propeller. *Lady Caroline* was a 42 ft sailboat made of ferrous cement, originally built in the UK. She was sailed out to the Caribbean as a cargo vessel. She was later purchased by an Antiguan who used her as a sailboat until she met her fate.

The *Erna*, a 443 ton iron barque, sank on 6 June 1900 on Belfast Reef, on the Atlantic side of the island in only 15 ft of water. Built in 1867 in Sunderland, she was crossing from Nantes, France to Mexico. Her last owner was C. P. Holm of Nordby, Denmark. Until the early 1920s, *Erna* was visible above sea level, but now all that remains is a broken hull in the shallow waters. In May 1989 the Antigua and Barbuda Historical Society hosted a snorkel field trip to the site and confirmed there were few remains left.

Most divers dream of chancing upon an ancient shipwreck and I am fortunate to have had such an encounter.

It took place at an unknown wreck site, although there is speculation that it could be the *Hope*, an American schooner arriving from Norfolk,

Virginia. The *Hope* sank in 1823. The site is now called the **Rickett Bottle Wreck**. It is thought, according to Teddy Tucker of Bermuda, that the vessel would have been a one-masted sailing sloop, around 65 ft long, with a crew of five or six. She was discovered by accident by my diving party during a pleasure dive on the northeast side of Antigua on 29 August 1987. She lies on sloping, shallow coral reef between 46 and 60 ft, indicating that she hit the reef and sank, tumbling down the coral incline.

**Peter Benchley and Teddy Tucker excavate the site of the Rickett Bottle Wreck**

On the day the *Rickett Bottle Wreck* was discovered, the diving party consisted of Dr Kelvin Charles, UK divers Lesley and Ian Runnalls, and myself. Ian Runnalls, an experienced wreck diver and salvor, noticed the coral was growing in a straight line and knew this was not normal. After closer investigation he discovered wood underneath the coral formation and recognised the timbers of an old shipwreck. An expedition was established, with the hope of recovering enough artefacts for a display at the Antigua and Barbuda Museum. Desmond Nicholson of the Historical Society was brought into this project in the initial days and the exploration was done on behalf of the museum.

Teddy Tucker, a treasure wreck diver from Bermuda, and writer Peter Benchley were invited to dive the site with me in October 1987. They determined that although it was not a treasure site, it would have some interesting historical significance. During the dive, Tucker uncovered a site on the wreck that provided evidence of dozens of glass bottles; although most were broken, one intact bottle was recovered and presented to Desmond Nicholson. Research, from the writing embossed on the base, indicated the bottles were from Bristol Glassworks, Bristol (England). 'H. Rickett' was also embossed on the base. In 1821 Henry Rickett patented his 'improvements in manufacturing glass bottles', and for the first time accurate dimensions and capacities of glass bottles could be made. The Rickett bottles achieved international fame and were sold throughout the world. Shiploads of bottles were sent to the United States, the West Indies and Australia. However, in 1857 Rickett Glassworks amalgamated with Powell and Filer and the bottle embossing was changed. Therefore it can be assumed that the shipwreck occurred between 1821 and 1860.

Earthenware pieces were also recovered and with the help of Isabella Hutchinson through Sothebys in New York, these were identified as Staffordshire earthenware, transfer-printed in underglaze blue with picturesque scenes. These were first produced around 1815 and continued to be made until the end of the 1860s, when they lost popularity. In the 1920s Wedgwood again produced similar pieces but the pottery identified from the site was felt to have been made around 1820 because of its thinness.

Other interesting items recovered included a badly damaged copper cooking pot, copper rivets and nails from 7 in to 9 in long, copper keel bolts from 26 to 30 in long, and a small stoneware pot, completely intact.

**A bronze keel bolt found on the site of the *Rickett Bottle Wreck***

Hurricanes Hugo in 1989 and Luis in 1995 interrupted the occasional exploration done on the site and for the time being examination of the wreck has ceased. It is hoped more excavation can be carried out, perhaps confirming the identify of this unknown vessel.

In 1987 there was an attempt at a major professional shipwreck salvage operation when the government of Antigua and Barbuda granted a 15-year licence to Mel Fisher's company Dreams Unlimited. Fisher's fame in wreck salvage was for his richest find – the *Nuestra Senora de Atocha* – a treasure laden seventeeth-century Spanish galleon sunk off the Florida Keys. Initially, being contracted by Fisher, the salvage boat *Shoreline XV* under Captain Chuck La Liberté arrived on Antigua operating on behalf of Seven Seas Salvage Inc. (owned by Swiss Tony Kopp). The salvage vessel *Riptide* replaced *Shoreline*, and worked until the end of 1989 when she left Antigua and Barbuda.

I have acted as the diving liaison officer for the Antigua and Barbuda Historical Society since the mid-1980s, to help represent and protect the rights of the society in any marine related matters. This led to my involvement with this venture, and I spent time with the salvage crew aboard *Riptide*.

## Barbuda

H. & E. Marine Enterprise Ltd determined that Barbuda, the lovely 'little sister island' of Antigua, had more potential in valuable treasure wrecks and so concentrated their salvage efforts there.

Two significant sites were discovered: a Spanish vessel thought to be the 1695 (?) wreck of the *Santiago de Cullerin*, and the HMS *Griffin*, a British warship.

The **Santiago de Cullerin** was wrecked on the east coast of Barbuda. Much mystery still remains about this site, as details have not been confirmed. Perhaps some day the evidence will be found to tell her true story. Treasure hunter Teddy Tucker from Bermuda also visited the site and after viewing the artefacts his expert opinion was that the ship sank between 1650 and 1700 on its way from Spain to the New World. Artefacts recovered from the site included olive jars, pieces of majolica with no colouring (this slipware was widely used by the Spanish and the earlier pieces had no colour, indicating an early wreck), lead oxide, spice seeds, small bits of leather, tar, creosote, and broken pieces of English plate dating from between 1660 and 1700.

Teddy Tucker and his daughter Wendy look on as the captain of the *Riptide* inspects a Spanish olive jar recovered on a Spanish wreck site off Barbuda

The corks found in some of the olive jars appeared to be new (with no nicks from being prised out, indicating that they had not been reused, as was the practice). When returning to Spain, the Spanish would ship New World items back to Spain, such as molasses, with the cork tops sealed with pitch found in the West Indies. No pitch was found on the cork tops, suggesting that the ship was probably not returning to Spain. Lead oxide was brought out to the New World, not taken back, so this would most likely not have been onboard if the ship had been returning to Spain. Olive seeds were found in the bottom of the olive jars. Olives brought across from Spain were totally consumed and because of the lengthy voyages there were no leftovers by the time the ship returned home – another indication that the ship was coming to the New World. This evidence is very significant because if the ship was on her outward voyage she would not have been laden with valuable treasures from South America. Thus the site is certainly of historical and archaeological value, but not a treasure site.

HMS *Griffin*, a heavily armed British warship, was part of the Seven Years War between 1756 and 1763 (King George's War). She sank on 27 October 1760, off a point of land known on early charts as Griffin Point. She was 118½ ft long, 34 ft wide and carried 28 guns. She was launched in England on 18 October 1758. She came to the West Indies on her maiden voyage with Captain Thomas Taylor in command. The cause of the accident was noted, in the official inquiry, as 'mistake in the reckoning occasioned by bad weather and unaccountable currents'. During the trial Captain Thomas Taylor's short statement was:

*On the 27 October being in chace of two French privateers, which we saw about 11 in the morning, and had continued until 9 in the evening, we saw the breakers of the outward shoals on the north east part of Barbuda and as we could not clear it, came to an anchor in five fathoms of water. In about 10 minutes the cables parted, then the ship fell off with her larboard broadside to the shoals when she heeled over and bilged, and in about 10 minutes she was entirely wrecked. I remained with her until next day after having sent all the other officers and men on shore and quitted her myself at 1 in the afternoon.*

Captain Taylor's court martial was held aboard the HMS *Culloden* and he and all officers and men were duly acquitted. The Museum of Antigua and Barbuda has copies of the extracts from the captain and master's logbooks of the HMS *Temple* that provide more insight into the events surrounding this.

In November 1988, H. & E. Marine Enterprises carried out research on this site, under contractual arrangements with Mel Fisher and the Antigua and Barbuda government. This revealed that a few weeks prior to her sinking, HMS *Griffin* and HMS *Temple* were engaged in heavy fighting with the French off Martinique. The two warships successfully recaptured HMS *Virgin*, and six French privateers. They also destroyed a number of coastal fortifications. From the archaeological data that H. & E. Marine Enterprises gathered during months of excavation on the site, the intensity and magnitude of the battles were evident. They documented cannon ball fragments and large numbers of grapeshot and also round musket shot, flattened from the impact. Over 3000 intact musket shot inspected were French military calibre (.69), probably confiscated from the French privateers captured. Many items recovered, including some pewter tankards, bore either the ship name or the stamp of the British broad arrow, indicating Crown property. Some of the artefacts recovered were turned over to the Barbuda Council and remain in their care.

Today remains can still be seen of this mighty warship which met such a violent ending. Thirteen cannon, stacks of pig iron ballast, gravel ballast and hundreds of encrusted cannon balls are scattered about the sandy seabed at 20 ft.

Another interesting wreck site on Barbuda is the site of the **Red Jacket**, an American Civil War blockade runner converted to a cargo boat. She hit the reef on Bailey Shoal, part of Cobb Reef, in 1863 and sank while carrying general cargo. The boiler is still visible.

Other significant sites include the SS **Croyden** (sank 1914), the SS **Polrose** (sank 1915) and the SS **Amersfoort** (sank 1927). It should be noted that sometimes in recording the locations of wrecks, mistakes were made. Wrecks recorded as having been sunk in Barbuda were actually sunk in Bermuda and vice versa!

As in Antigua, the water is very shallow around Barbuda, so one can easily enjoy good snorkelling. Ancient anchors and evidence of some of the wrecks mentioned, or others, can be seen easily by snorkellers.

While Antigua and Barbuda are not actively promoted as major wreck diving locations, given the history of ships wrecked around the islands there is always the chance, as happened to me, of coming upon an ancient shipwreck!

Divers should remember, however, that these sites are protected by the 1972 Marine Areas Act, and should explore them without disturbing the historical remains.

# Barbados

1. SS *Stavronikita*
2. *Berwyn*
3. *Ce-Trek*
4. *Marian Bell Wolfe*
5. *Granny* or *Boiler Wreck*
   (locally called *Martha's Wreck*)
6. *Lord Combermere*
7. *Lord Willoughby*
8. *Friars Craig*
9. *Pamir*
10. *Cuban Wreck*
11. *Countess of Ripon*

Barbados, one of the more developed and sophisticated islands of the Eastern Caribbean, has a wide range of leisure activities on offer. It is therefore ideal for the diver who wants to do more than dive, or for the diver travelling with a non-diving companion. If exploring, enjoying local dining spots and experiencing a bit of the nightlife are appealing, this island is the perfect choice.

As well as offering reef diving, Barbados has become known as a destination for the exciting alternative of wreck diving, with a number of interesting wrecks to explore. Several of them have been sunk intentionally as diving sites.

The largest and probably best known wreck is the SS **Stavronikita**, a 356 ft Greek cargo ship. The '*Stav*', as she is called by those who know her, was built in Denmark in 1956. In her early days she sailed under the name of *Ohio*, but this was changed in 1971 to *Vasia*, according to Lloyds Registry of Shipping in London. She was later renamed the *Stavronikita*, and carried cargo throughout the world until 26 August

The sinking of the
*Stavronikita*

1976, when she caught fire off Barbados while carrying cement. Her owners never expected this to be her final voyage. The fire started at approximately 6 a.m. in the chief engineer's cabin and swept through the ship. When the flames finally abated, six men were dead and three injured. The *Stavronikita* was out of commission and drifting! Two Barbados tugs, the *Barbados* and the *Culpepper*, came to her rescue on 1 September  and towed the charred remains back to Barbados. It was these same two tugs which eventually towed her to her final

**The top side of the *Stavronikita* on the day of sinking**

**Martha Watkins Gilkes explores the *Stavronikita*** (George Hume)

resting place, where she now lies in 130 ft of water.

After two years of debate on the fate of the *Stav* she was bought by the Barbados Tourist Board to be sunk as a diving site in the Barbados Marine Reserve, an underwater park where legislation prevents careless divers from taking any marine objects. This gave the *Stav* a safe resting place where she could grow into a beautiful wreck site for divers of the future. The main marine growth is in the more shallow depths, however, as deeper water and limited sunlight do not encourage the development of marine life. The enormous size of the *Stav* (she has a gross tonnage of 4129 tons) and her intact superstructure make her a wreck diver's dream and there is unlimited subject matter for the underwater photographer. The *Stav* has four large cargo holds and the massive main mast and derrick support ascend from the top deck in about 80 ft of water, to within 15 ft of the surface. She originally had 12 winches and 14 cargo derricks and although some of the machinery was stripped, much was left intact. The massive propeller is still attached, and although in deep water (125 ft), it is a luring attraction.

Underwater film maker Stan Waterman filming on the *Stavronikita*

The *Stavronikita* came to her final resting place on 22 November 1978 about 400 yards off the west coast of Barbados near Prospect, St James, when she was dynamited with some 200 pounds of explosives. A US Navy team from Puerto Rico carefully placed the explosives at strategic points on the ship and directed the sinking. At approximately 12.35 p.m., with onlookers lining the beaches, the first explosion went off. The *Stav* immediately began to sink and after six explosions, in 13 minutes and 3 seconds, it was all over. She went down, as planned, on her keel and sits upright. She can only be viewed by scuba divers now!

However, the *Stav* is not forgotten. As well as being visited by countless divers on a regular basis, she has been written up in numerous magazines. In 1980 a documentary film was made by well-known American cinematographer Stan Waterman. Her 'sea change' has made her a beauty to behold, with black coral trees now adorning her decks and schools of colourful reef fish making her their home.

For some time the *Stav* had one unique inhabitant, a friendly barracuda locally known as George. George took up residence on the shipwreck some years ago, and began to behave in an extraordinary way. He would hang vertically, at 95 ft, within a passageway of the *Stav*, admiring his reflection in a large air bubble, caused by the exhalation of divers breathing compressed air (see p. 14). This bubble, trapped in the ceiling, acted as a mirror and attracted George. For several years divers had a unique opportunity of observing a barracuda close up; unfortunately he is no longer seen on the site.

A word of warning on diving the *Stav*: she lies in deep water and is considered an advanced dive. She is not safe for the inexperienced diver, so don't consider visiting her unless you are experienced. For those capable of such a dive, the site is a must on a diving trip to Barbados. Most of the dive shops on the island will arrange dives to the wreck, although these may not be on a daily basis, so arrangements should be made in advance.

Another well-known wreck site and one that is easy to dive is the **Berwyn**, located in Carlisle Bay. The *Berwyn* is a World War I French tug which sank in 1919 and is now totally encrusted in coral. There is a host of small colourful reef fish all around the wreck. She lies in only 25 ft of water, with the top deck being only about 10 ft from the surface, making her an ideal snorkelling site also. The *Berwyn* is about 50 ft long and is perfect for a beginner's dive or as the first dive of the year for a diver who has had a break from diving. She is easily accessible from the beach or from a boat hired from one of the diving shops. Schools of hungry sergeant majors and yellowtail snappers abound and are always on hand, hoping for a handout from divers. Much of the upper structure of the wreck has begun to break up as she lies in shallow water and has been damaged by wave action. In addition, much harm has been done by inconsiderate boaters who drop their anchors near the structure and carelessly damage the wreck.

**Martha Watkins Gilkes exploring the inside of the wreck of the *Berwyn*** (Steve Birchall)

In February 1987 the **Ce-Trek**, a 45 ft long Barbados based ice-fishing boat, was sunk just south of the *Berwyn* in 40 ft of water. As she is only a five-minute swim from the *Berwyn*, divers can explore both wrecks on one dive. The *Ce-Trek* was sunk in the Careenage, where she lay for two weeks before being lifted and moved to her present location. She is a concrete boat, and has attracted much growth. The wooden cabin is slowly deteriorating, but the main structure remains intact. A family of lobsters enjoys the shelter of her leeward side.

The interior of the wreck of the *Berwyn* in 1985

Carlisle Bay offers three other known wreck diving sites, although a study of the archives reveals that there are at least 12 other ships in the bay, which was the original anchorage for the island. These ships are just waiting to be discovered by some lucky diver! The **Marian Bell Wolfe**, locally called the *Wolfe*, is a wooden structure lying in 40 ft of water to the north of the *Berwyn*. The *Wolfe* was built in Nova Scotia. She sailed around the waters of Saba as well as plying the seas between Guyana and Barbados. She spent her later days around the Southern Caribbean and in September 1955 she was damaged by Hurricane Janet. She eventually sank at anchor in Carlisle Bay where she now lies. Although rather broken up and perhaps not nearly as interesting to dive on as the more intact wrecks, she does attract schools of fish.

The **Granny**, also called the *Boiler Wreck* and known locally by divers as *Martha's Wreck*, lies in 45 ft of water to the north of the *Wolfe*. It is said that she was transferring drums of gasoline to another vessel when an explosion sank her. Only a part of the metal structure is still visible, but what there is affords a rich variety of marine life, with a very large resident green moray; turtles are often spotted. Divers have also seen manta rays gracefully gliding by – a real underwater treat.

An added attraction to diving the wrecks of Carlisle Bay is hunting for antique bottles. Carlisle Bay was the anchorage for seventeenth- and eighteenth-century ships and a profusion of bottles are waiting to be discovered: wine bottles of many types and ages, assorted stoneware bottles, mineral water bottles of various shapes, and marble bottles. Since Barbados was British until the 1960s, many of the bottles are of British origin. An authoritative book on antique bottles would be a good item to pack for a Barbados diving holiday!

Up the west coast of the island, *Lord Combermere* and *Lord Willoughby* rest. **Lord Combermere** is a metal tugboat that was sunk intentionally around 1974. Some say she was water tender to a larger boat. Locally she is called the 'Shallow Wreck' and sits upright on a slope that gently falls from 30 to 50 ft off Batts Rock on the west coast. The hold is easily accessible through an opening on her deck. An added treat when exploring *Lord Combermere* is the sight of a school of graceful garden eels, swaying in currents just off the prop on the nearby sandy 60 ft bottom.

**Lord Willoughby**, probably named after one of the former governors of the island, is also an old water barge, approximately 60 ft long. She was sunk around 1975, also intentionally as a diving site. She is located just off Clarkes Reef, in about 100 ft of water.

In July 1985 two new wrecks were sunk intentionally: the *Friars Craig* and *Pamir*.

The **Friars Craig** is a 160 ft, 590 ton freighter built in Holland in 1938. For ten years she sat at anchor, unused, in Carlisle Bay until the Barbados port authority finally decided that she was a hazard to other ships in the bay, as her rusty anchor chain might break in rough seas. The decision to sink her was made, with the consent of her owner, and on 2 July 1985 she came to rest in 50 ft of water, on a sandy bottom at latitude 13° 04' 78 N on the south coast of Barbados, just outside Carlisle Bay. She is fringed on the shore side by a 30 ft reef and on the starboard side by a 60 ft reef. Before she was sunk holes were cut in her sides to allow divers to swim safely inside the hull. The mast and crane boom were cut and secured to the hatch. Most of the engine room was left intact and the prop remains. There was already ten years of growth on her prop when she went down as a result of her long anchorage in

*(opposite)*
**Martha Watkins Gilkes**
**on the bow of the**
***Friars Craig***
*(George Hume)*

**Martha Watkins Gilkes
descends inside the *Pamir***
*(George Hume)*

the bay, making her an ideal site for photography. Since she was sunk, some wave action has damaged the structure and she has actually broken up, but she is still an interesting dive site and a shallow reef dive can also be incorporated in the dive plan.

The *Pamir*, a 150 ft motor vessel, was sunk off the west coast of Barbados on 19 July 1985. She sank in 50 ft of water in only 15 minutes after her seacocks were opened. Schools of blue chromis and blackbar solider fish congregate within her structure, and, like the *Stav*, she is undergoing a 'sea change' into a beautiful wreck for divers to enjoy.

The ships I have mentioned as diving sites in this chapter are all from the twentieth century but, as for the other Caribbean islands, tales abound of ancient wrecks, perhaps with treasure still onboard!

Every diver dreams of finding a gold-laden treasure ship. While no one can boast of this yet in the waters off Barbados, there are records of over 70 wrecks that sank between 1666 and 1872. Twelve of these wrecks are said to be in Carlisle Bay, with the majority of the remainder being on the east coast of the island.

A possible interesting wreck was mentioned by Mr Edward Stoute, well known Barbadian historian, in a newspaper article on 20 June 1976. Mr Stoute said that a steamer broke her prop shaft when entering Carlise Bay in 1872 and sank; she became known as the *Cuban Wreck*. No one can determine her exact location but one day some lucky diver may stumble upon her, making yet another known wreck site for Barbados.

The famed Sam Lord of Barbados is reputed to have hung lanterns in the coconut trees off his castle on the rough east coast of the island, luring ships onto the shallow reefs and then looting them. However, Sam Lord may be blamed for more than he deserves. He occupied the castle (today a hotel) from 1820 to 1844 and only nine ships are reported to have sunk on Cobblers Reef, the reef directly off the castle, during that period.

Another eighteenth-century shipwreck lies on the east coast, but few know the location. *The Countess of Ripon* sank in 1866 when she hit a reef off Skeete's Bay. She was a new iron ship of 1209 tons and was coming from India to St Vincent. Today her brass bell can be seen at the Barbados Turf Club – a tribute to the memory of this sailing lady of the past.

There are probably many other such ancient wrecks off the coast of Barbados, but all the evidence that we have is a note in the archives.

Diving in Barbados is much safer than in some Caribbean destinations. The island has a decompression chamber, used for treating diving accidents. The chamber is owned and operated by the Barbados Defense Force with assistance from the Eastern Caribbean Safe Diving

**Donna Hume on the wreck of the** *Pamir*
*(George Hume)*

The *Pamir* (George Hume)

Association (ECSDA), an organisation of safety-minded volunteers who helped raise funds to install the chamber in January 1985. Although a diver never plans to get bend, the availability of a chamber is an added safety factor for scuba diving. In addition, ECSDA has established minimum safe operating standards for diving shops on the island; Barbados is one of the few islands to have such safety standards. The system is a self-imposed one, and not all diving establishments adhere to it. It is a good idea to confirm which shops are safety minded before planning a diving vacation with them.

**Martha Watkins Gilkes, then President of the Eastern Caribbean Safe Diving Association, at the decompression chamber in Barbados**

Exciting wrecks to explore, high safety standards and the facilities of a well-developed island make Barbados an excellent choice for the scuba diver who does not necessarily want to 'get away from it all'.

# The British Virgin Islands

1. RMS *Rhone*
2. *Chikuzen*
3. *Inganess Bay*
4. *Marie L*
5. *The Pat*
6. *Barge and Grill*
7. *Fearless*
8. HMS *Astrea*
9. *Rocus*

Tales abound about the shipwrecks around the British Virgin Islands, especially on the Anegada Reef. It has been said there are more than 350 wrecks on this shallow reef alone. Over 150 have been documented, although most have never been located. There are certainly some that are of great archaeological significance.

The jewel in the crown of wreck diving in the British Virgin Islands is the RMS **Rhone**. Regarded by many as the most beautiful shipwreck in the Caribbean, this nineteenth-century steam packet is certainly the best-known dive site in the BVIs. *Skin Diver* magazine has dubbed the *Rhone* the best diving wreck in the Caribbean!

The Millwall Iron Works in England built the *Rhone* in 1867 for the Royal Mail Steam Packet Company. She was 310 ft long, had a beam of 40 ft, and could reach an impressive speed of 12 knots. Although steam driven, she also carried two large steel masts and square rigged sails.

The *Rhone* and her sister ship the RMS *Douro* were both to have short lives, although the *Rhone*'s demise was more tragic and violent. The *Douro* sank in the Bay of Biscay in 500 ft after a collision with another vessel. She was carrying a fortune in gold and diamonds. Her location was unknown until the 1990s when salvage divers located her in a remotely operated vehicle and recovered most of her gold.

The RMS *Rhone* sank under the command of Captain Wooley during a late season hurricane on 29 October 1867. On that fateful day Captain Wooley noted that his barometer was standing at 30 in. He commented to the commander of the RMS *Packet Conway* that he did not like the look of the weather. Captain Wooley had planned to shift anchorage to the Northern Islands, but before he could take action the weather turned and the *Rhone* began to drag anchor. She attempted to get to sea but was driven backwards against the rocky point of Salt Island, 5½ miles from Tortola. There were 147 passengers and crew aboard; only one Italian passenger and 22 crew survived. Although many were drowned, many others were killed when the steam boiler exploded. Four crewmen survived by clinging to the rigging, which remained above the water after the ship was driven onto the rocks. She went to the bottom carrying a fortune in gold – over $60,000 US.

The rigging also allowed a quick salvage operation, as the site was easy to locate. Salvage diver Jeremiah Murphy of the Turk Islands and his two brothers were employed for $20,000 to salvage the wreck, arriving soon after the hurricane. Within four years both brothers drowned – one in the hold of the *Liverpool Packet* in St Thomas harbour and the other while diving on the British steamer *Columbia* also at the entrance of St Thomas harbour.

Amusing stories are recorded about the salvage operation. One account in the *Port of Spain Gazette* (Trinidad), tells of a visit by friends of Murphy to the salvage site. He had been diving on one of the two pieces of wreckage and surfaced in time to dine. He advised the ladies he had nothing 'good to offer them' and that he would dive down again and search the other part of the ship, in spite of their objections.

*Within the half hour he produced as much champagne, beer, soda water, lemonade, seltz water and brandy as we knew what to do with, the liquors were as good as they were the first day and it is nearly three years since they have been down. The champagne was first rate, as cool as possible, we drank it out of tumblers as we did not have champagne glasses.*

The *Rhone* has been lying on the seabed for over 130 years, and in that time she has become a Hollywood star. The 1979 Columbia Pictures film *The Deep*, starring Jacqueline Bissett and Nick Nolte and

based on Peter Benchley's story of treasure diving, used the *Rhone* as the treasure wreck and made her famous! For a time it also popularised wet tee shirt diving as Jacqueline Bissett chose this as her diving attire! Underwater film maker Stan Waterman, who worked on the shoot, commented, 'When Jacqueline exited the water strong men would sob aloud!'

Benchley returned for additional filming on the *Rhone* in 1986. He commented that she was a world class wreck – deep enough to be an exciting dive, mature enough to have tremendous growth and inhabited by numerous fish, including two enormous jewfish. To avid wreck divers, nearly any shipwreck is exciting. To dive on a ship that has been down for so many years, has a vivid known history and is covered with invertebrate life and an abundance of fish life, is a particularly rewarding experience.

The *Rhone* is now part of the 798 acre Rhone Marine Park, which gives her a safe resting place and preserves her for future divers to enjoy

The *Rhone*'s structure is covered in a profusion of marine growth, as she has been lying in the warm tropical waters for over 130 years

**Marine organisms, a variety of corals and invertebrate life have claimed the structure of the *Rhone* as home, making her come alive again**

and explore. Her remains lie along a sloping reef with depths ranging from 15 to 80 ft, so allowing divers at all levels of experience to dive the site. The dive shops usually dive the *Rhone* as a double dive, with the deeper section being explored first.

In 1989 Hurricane Hugo uncovered human bones on the site, which were buried on nearby Salt Island. A plaque was placed on the burial site reading 'A hurricane took me down; a hurricane brought me up'.

The rear half of the vessel is scattered across the bottom but the forward 150 ft of the wreck is intact, lying on its starboard side. More than twelve decades of submersion under the sea have transformed the wreck into a magnificent, coral-covered structure carpeted with hard corals, sea fans, tube sponges and numerous varieties of marine life. The wreck is inhabited by an enormous number of fish, including squirlfish, parrot fish and several dozen species of reef fish. The giant jewfish mentioned by Benchley hide under the bow. Because of her proximity to the open sea the *Rhone* attracts all sorts of pelagic life, including threadfin pompano, tarpon and tuna.

The site is a photographer's paradise for both wide angle and macro

*(opposite)*
**A diver explores a plaque from RMS *Rhone***

*(opposite)*
**The *Rhone* carried
two cannon; one lies in
70 feet of water and is
covered in marine growth**

lenses, as the cavernous interior of the hull is covered with orange tubasterea cup corals which extend their yellow polyps even in daylight hours. All dive shops in the BVIs dive the *Rhone* and know the wreck well, giving excellent guided tours.

Another unique site for the wreck diver, now considered to be the next best wreck in the BVIs after the *Rhone*, is the wreck of the **Chikuzen**, a 246 ft steel hull ship, originally part of a Korean fishing fleet. There are conflicting reports on her actual date of sinking. Most sources say she sank in August 1981 (some say September). Ken Turbe of St Thomas declares it was 1983, as he was working in the BVIs and witnessed her burning. *Indepth* (October 1990) says she was in port in 1982, entangled in legal battles.

Originally a longline fishing boat, the *Chikuzen* spent her final days as a cold storage facility, tied up alongside a dock in St Martin. As her engines no longer operated, she had to be removed from the dock and she was taken out to sea to be sunk. Her seacocks were open, but, reluctant to sink, she drifted some 70 miles until she finally went down at her present location in the Sir Francis Drake Channel.

She lies in 75 ft of water on her port side on a sandy bottom 8 miles north of Great Camanoe Island near Virgin Gorda. She is also located on the migratory path of humpback whales, and divers often hear their song as they pass. The area abounds in other pelagic creatures such as sharks, eagle rays, cobias and jewfish.

Sandflats surround the wreck. Because of her size, location and the fact that she has been down for nearly two decades, she is an exciting diving site and has attracted abundant marine life. Large (200 lb) groupers, schools of horse-eye jacks and barracudas, and an occasional shark maybe spotted. The top deck rests at 40 ft and thorny oystershells and a variety of marine creatures cover the hull.

The Chikuzen's location means that she is best dived in calm seas, and even then it takes over an hour to reach the site. However, for the more experienced diver, this is an enthralling wreck dive.

The 350 ton, 146 ft **Inganess Bay** was a victim of Hurricane Bertha, which hit the BVIs in July 1996.

Just before the hurricane she was in port in St Thomas and the US coast guard ordered the crew to remove her from any US port. As the hurricane was already developing, Captain Cosmos Sealey from Grenada had to head for the nearest safe port; he felt this was Tortola. The crew rode out the first half of the hurricane but during the second

half the engine could not keep up with the fierce winds and when the anchor chain snapped, the ship was driven ashore on the rocks by the Moorings Marina. Fortunately, no one was injured.

This was the second time *Inganess Bay* had been the victim of a hurricane. In 1989 she was washed ashore on Blake Island off Antigua. The very day this happened she had just been repaired after a major breakdown off Guadeloupe. Her owner, Hugh Bailey, told how he had rescued her and towed her back to Antigua; the engines were repaired on the day Hurricane Hugo was coming. It was too late to take her down island out of the storm path. However, the damage was not serious and she, along with another vessel he owned, were pulled off.

The *Inganess Bay* started life as the *Wiser Grief*. She was built in Holland in 1951 and for some years operated in the Shetland Islands, carrying grain. Hugh Bailey purchased her for approximately £60,000 in 1980 from Herbert Shipping and sailed her with a crew from the UK, arriving in Antigua in July 1980. She operated very success-fully for many years as one of the first large cargo ships based out of Antigua.

She had some narrow escapes during her life. Around 1986 she was heavily loaded with school buses and trucks bound for Grenada from Puerto Rico. She developed a serious list from a leak and Hugh Bailey took her into St Croix. Part of the heavy cargo had to be offloaded and left behind until a future trip. In late 1989, according to Hugh Bailey, the *Inganess Bay* was sold to three Grenadians who continued to operate her as a cargo ship between Puerto Rico and Trinidad, until her demise in the 1996 hurricane. Bailey was still owed some $25,000 US but commented that he never pursued it as the owners also lost much money in the tragedy and there was no insurance.

After she was washed ashore the crew saved some of the cargo and some parts of the vessel were removed. The wheel was returned to Hugh Bailey as a memento. She lay on the shore for some time until the owners finally donated her to the BVI Dive Operators' Association. According to Joe Giacinto, president of the Association, various meetings were held with the ports authority, the Department of Conservation and Fisheries, local police and the fire brigade. A location out of the shipping lanes and away from boating traffic was finally decided for her. The Association made arrangements to have her prepared for the sinking. Her fuel tanks were emptied, the engines were taken out and most of the doors were removed. Captain Sealey, her last captain, and his crew did much of the labour for this. *Inganess Bay* was pulled off and towed to her final resting place in August 1996.

Kevin Rolette, owner of Shanty Maritime Services Ltd, provided assistance and the expertise for the removal and sinking, a task which turned out to be much more complicated than had been anticipated. The job was started at 6 a.m. but the vessel was not floated until noon. It took ten pumps working full time to keep her afloat until she could be towed from Roadtown harbour to Cooper Island, a one-hour tow. Finally at 3.30 p.m. she sank beneath the waves to her present resting place in 95 ft of water.

Hurricane damage to the *Inganess Bay* did not end even when she rested on the bottom of the sea. Hurricane Georges in 1998 moved her and broke up the wreck. Nevertheless, the wreck is an interesting diving site and stands witness to the continuity of life despite the violent hurricanes that hit the region: she has now become a home for countless marine creatures.

The **Marie L** is a 75 ft freighter that lies in 45–90 ft of water off Cooper Island. She was a locally owned cargo boat bought by Winston Leonard of Leonard's Shipping from the government at an auction after she had been confiscated in the late 1970s for drug running. He used her to run cargo between the BVIs and Puerto Rico for some years. After breaking down, she sat at the government dock for some time; a hurricane was approaching and there was concern that she would cause damage, so it was decided to remove her and sink her. However in the end the hurricane never hit! Blue Waters Divers sank the *Marie L* in the early 1990s as a diving site. She rests on a sandy bottom just off a small coral wall.

The **Pat**, a 70 ft tug, lies right next to the *Marie L*, bow to stern, in the same depth. Owned by Moses Malone from West End, she was used for towing sand barges. She was sunk by Underwater Safaris around 1995. On her descent to the bottom, she struck the *Marie L* and slid off her.

Close to these two wrecks divers can find a large colony of garden eels living in the sand. Stingrays are also often seen in the area.

Also in the same area lies the **Barge and Grill,** owned by a Mr Casey who used her within the islands. Rumour has it that a hammer was dropped through the hull and repairs were never made. Blue Waters Divers sank her in the mid-1980s. This site has been badly broken up by adverse weather and is rarely dived now.

The *Fearless* is a 100 ft fishing trawler that lies in 80 ft of water off Peter Island, in the entrance to Great Harbor. She sank in 1986 in a state of disrepair. The *Willie T* was sunk around 1999 next to the *Fearless*. She had been a popular bar and restaurant boat anchored in the Norman Island Bight.

Horseshoe Reef, off Anegada, has claimed hundreds of shipwrecks over the years. Tage and Charlotte Blytmann have documented around 150 of these wrecks dating between 1523 and 1899 on their website www.blytmann.com/anegada.htm. The earliest is a Spanish ship wrecked in 1523.

Of the more ancient sites, an especially interesting one well researched and documented by Tage Blytmann is the HMS *Astrea*. This 140 ft fifth-rate 32 gun British frigate was wrecked off Anegada on 23 May 1808 while under the command of Captain Edward Heywood. She was carrying a crew of 220 men and officers, but only four lives were lost when she sank.

One of eight new fifth-rate frigates built in 1778, she was launched in 1781 and named after the goddess of justice, the daughter of Zeus and the last divinity to leave earth when the Golden Age had passed. She had an interesting career throughout the West Indies from 1796. She took part in the capture of St Lucia, St Vincent and Grenada from the French. In 1967, 160 years after the tragedy of her sinking, she was

**An early engraving of the *Rhone***

THE ROYAL MAIL STEAM PACKET RHONE

discovered by an ambitious group of divers who had carefully researched her whereabouts. Others had searched for her unsuccessfully for many years. The diving team consisted of Dr Orlin Rice, Dr David Berglund, Captain Ralph Gresens and Captain Bert Kilbride. They had been assisted with much research done on the potential location by Tage Blytmann, although he was not able to be part of the diving team. Tage Blytmann has documented the history of the loss, along with a summary of the court martial, on his website; there is also a detailed account of her rediscovery and salvage efforts (www.blytmann.com, under Astrea).

One of the more modern wrecks on the Anegada Reef is the **Rocus**, a 380 ft iron Greek freighter that went down in 1929. The ship was carrying animal bones for fertiliser (and so has been dubbed the *Bone Wreck*) and these are now scattered across the seabed, making for a rather eerie site. She was en route from Trinidad to Baltimore. The actual structure of the wreck is broken up as it is very exposed to the wind and the sea and lies in only 15–35 ft. However, divers can easily see the engines, a large 20 ft boiler, winches and a capstan. It is not dived a great deal, perhaps because of restrictions on anchoring in less than 45 ft of water on the Anegada Reef.

The BVIs are particularly rich in stories of ancient shipwrecks, and have much to offer the wreck diver. Further information can be found in *Diving British Virgin Islands*, by Jim and Odile Scheiner (Aqua Quest Publications, 1997).

The author interviewing
Dr David Berglund
about his many years of
shipwreck exploration in
the British Virgin Islands.
The painting in the
background shows
the *Rhone*
*(Charlotte Berglund)*

For a 45 minute video tape of a dive by Armando Jenik on the wreck of the *Rhone*, contact:

    Sea 3D Productions
    PO Box 9968
    St Thomas
    US Virgin Islands

For a detailed historical chart of RMS *Rhone*, contact:

    Wavey Line Publishing
    PO Box 101
    Grand Turk
    Turks and Caicos
    BWI
    *fax* 649 946 1059   *telephone* 649 941 6009

# The Cayman Islands

**Grand Cayman:**

1. *Doc Poulson Wreck*
2. *Oro Verde*
3. *Carrie Lee*
4. *Kirk Pride*
5. LCM *David Nicholson*
6. *Ridgefield*
7. *Rimandi Mibaju*
8. *Mary Belle*
9. *Methuselah*
10. *Balboa*
11. *Pallas*
12. *Cali*
13. *Arbutus*
14. *Wanderer IX*
15. *Geneva Kathleen*
16. *Ten Sail Wreck*

**Cayman Brac:**

17. *Kissimee*
18. *Cayman Mariner*
19. *Buccaneer*
20. *Captain Keith Tibbetts*
21. *Prince Frederick*

**Little Cayman:**

22. *Soto Trader*

*(opposite)*
**The Oro Verde**

The Cayman Islands boast a large array of shipwrecks. Fortunately these sites are protected from pilferage, as the Cayman Islands have been involved in the study and documentation of their shipwrecks for some years. The historical shipwrecks in the Cayman waters that have been down for more than 50 years are all protected under the Abandoned Wreck Law and ownership is 'vested

in Her Majesty in right of Her Government of the Islands'. In 1979 the Cayman Island government made a very innovative move: it invited professional underwater archaeologists through the Institute of Nautical Archaeology (INA) to come to the Caymans and document the shipwrecks. Seventy-five ancient wrecks were recorded in that study. According Dr Margaret E. Leshikar-Denton, these include the seventeenth-century 'Turtle Wreck', an English turtle-fishing vessel thought to have been burned in 1670 by a Spanish privateer, Manuel Rivero Pardal; the 'Careening Place', a rich site known from at least the early eighteenth century; possible remains of vessels lost in the 1794 'Wreck of the Ten Sail'; and wrecks from the nineteeth and twentieth centuries. Many of the ancient sites are not recognisable as shipwrecks owing to deterioration; they are often in hostile locations and are not suitable for sport divers. Therefore, although they are of interest and are fascinating, they are not dived for pleasure. The National Museum of the Cayman Islands has the responsibility of carrying out any archaeological research on these sites, assuring their preservation and protection.

There are plenty of other sites to choose from for the enthusiastic wreck diver. Among the modern wrecks the newest important dive site, located at Cayman Brac, is the wreck of the *Captain Keith Tibbetts*, the project of diving entrepreneur Wayne Hasson. The Brac also boasts the wrecks of the *Cayman Mariner*, the *Kissimee*, the *Prince Frederick* and the *Buccaneer*. On Grand Cayman the wrecks include the *Doc Poulson*, *Oro Verde*, the *Balboa*, the LCM *David Nicholson*, the *Cali*, the *Ridgefield*, the *Pallas*, the *Kirk Pride*, the *Carrie Lee*, the *Wanderer IX* and the *Geneva Kathleen*. More ancient sites include the *Rimandi Mibaju*, the *Mary Belle*, the *Methuselah*, the *Arbutus II* and the *Ten Sail Wreck*. Little Cayman is also not without its wrecks: the *Soto Trader* lies in these waters.

## Grand Cayman

The **Doc Poulson Wreck** was a tugboat built in Japan, with all its instruments and gauges in Japanese. She was used to dig the channel for a yacht club. After she had lived out her usefulness it was decided to sink her. She was partially sunk and sitting on the bottom and had to be pumped out to be moved. At 6 a.m. on the day of sinking in March 1991, the *Doc Poulson* was towed around to Seven Mile Beach by the *Cayman Aggressor* and according to Wayne Hasson, of the *Aggressor* fleet, three anchors were placed to hold her in the desired location, with her stern pointing northwest. She was then flooded and sank below the

The MV *Captain Keith Tibbetts* in port in Cuba before being taken to the Cayman Islands for sinking
*(Wayne Hasson)*

waterline to the top of her deck. However, she refused to go below the waterline! Boats could pull alongside and their crew could stand on the top deck. According to Hasson, Adrian Briggs, a long-time dive operator in the Caymans, climbed aboard, fully clothed; at that moment she sank below the waterline, just before sunset! It had taken all day to get her to the bottom of the sea. The wreck is named for a late doctor who did major work with the hyperbaric recompression chamber at the local hospital. This 100 ft vessel lies in 55 ft of water on a sand patch surrounded by live coral and garden eels. Her propeller is covered in colourful growth and the wreck offers many good photographic sites.

The wreck of the 181 ft **Oro Verde** (Spanish for 'green gold') is among the best-known Grand Cayman wrecks. This is not surprising, as she was the first wreck sunk on Grand Cayman on 31 May 1980, by a group of dive operators. Hurricane Allen in 1980 moved the wreck about 100 yards, according to Wayne Hasson. The *Oro Verde* is the sister ship of the SS *Pueblo*, famous for spying missions during the Korean and Vietnam wars. *Oro Verde* was first named the SS *Navajo*. After she was retired the Green Banana Trading Company bought her and she was used for shipping cargo for some years.

Later it seems she was being used as a drug running boat and had run aground on a reef on the north side of the island. The crew knew they

Divers Stan and Conner Huckaby, Ambassador Tom Anderson and Ted Bratrud around the propeller of the *Doc Poulson*

Martha Watkins Gilkes on the wreck of the *Oro Verde* (Richard McCrea)

would be caught, so they abandoned her. She was sunk in 40 to 56 ft of water. She has been broken up by storms and so is not intact.

The 100 ft container ship **Carrie Lee** is a deep wreck; the depth ranges from 130 to 200 ft. She flipped over in a bad storm on the south side of the island while under way to the Sister Islands with cargo. She was towed around to George Town, but was taking on water and sank before she could reach safety. All the crew members were rescued.

The 175 ft **Kirk Pride** sank in 1976. She was a freighter and developed mechanical problems while she was loading freight at the main dock in Cayman. The weather turned foul and the *Kirk Pride* could not get out of the harbour. Her clutch was not working and the engine had to be started with her gears in reverse. She eventually ended up on the rocks. Bob Sota's dive boat then pulled her off the rocks and anchors were set over the wall drop-off to hold her in place. The water was being pumped out but the pumps could not keep up and the *Kirk Pride* started to sink. Then the wind shifted and she swung over the drop-off, where she disappeared! Divers searched for her in up to 200 ft of water with no success. Finally in 1986 the *Atlantis* submarine spotted her sitting on an 800 ft ledge. Now she may only be observed from the portholes of the *Atlantis*, which runs trips for visitors.

Off the waters of Sunset House resort, about 200 yards from the shore, lie the remains of the LCM **David Nicholson**, a 50 ft World War II landing craft. She was sunk in April 1990 and is named after the late David Nicholson, a French Canadian and pioneer of diving in Cayman waters who worked at Sunset House. The wreck lies in 55 ft of water.

The rusting remains of the **Ridgefield** are located 300 yards south of the main channel to East End Sound. The New England Shipbuilding Company built this 2500 ton steel liberty ship in 1943 in Portland, Maine. She was originally named the *James A. Butts* and then had four other names during her life. She had a close call serving in the Pacific in World War II when she was narrowly missed by a Japanese torpedo. She was a victim of the shallow barrier reef on the East End of Grand Cayman. She lies, badly broken up, in shallow water of only 3–15 ft. Her massive 15 ft propeller and large steam engine can still be seen. There is also evidence of an earlier wreck lying under the *Ridgefield*. There is an interesting account of a visit aboard the *Ridgefield* after she ran upon the reef by George Hudson in *An Adventurer's Guide to the Unspoiled Cayman Islands*.

On the East End of Grand Cayman lies the *Rimandi Mibaju*. The *Mary Belle* and the *Methuselah* are also located in this area.

The 240 ft **Rimandi Mibaju**, also called the *Bauxite Wreck*, was a twentieth-century freighter that carried bauxite. She was on a cargo run from Surinam when she ran aground in 1964. This 2400 ton steel freighter was built in Superior, Wisconsin, originally to be used in the Great Lakes area. She sank in 1980 and lies in shallow water (16–33 ft) on the windward side of the island north of the main channel to East End Sound, just outside Windward Reef. There is not a great deal left on the wreck but one can see the boiler, ribs and engines. The large propeller is still attached.

Nearby on this shallow site, between 12 and 40 ft, the **Mary Belle** and the **Methuselah** lie on top of each other. The *Mary Belle* was a steel steamship and the *Methuselah* was a steel sailing boat with three masts. There is little history known about these two wrecks. As it is so shallow, this is a good snorkelling site when the water is calm.

The lumber steamer **Balboa** sank just north of George Town harbour in 1932 while at anchor during a hurricane. The wreck was a shipping hazard, so in 1957 it was blasted to try to protect boats in the area. The wreckage was strewn over a large area. The 375 ft wreck lies in only 26–33 ft and makes an excellent night dive, as she is very encrusted with marine life. There are discussions on moving the ship to make way for an extension to George Town harbour. It is hoped that if this is done the parts of the wreck will be kept as intact as possible.

The **Pallas** was driven upon a reef in Norwegian Bay in South Sound on 12 and 13 October 1910, in a hurricane with winds of 80–85 mph. Fortunately the captain and crew were saved. Many of the broken parts of the ship are now incorporated into the homes of the people living along the South Sound. When she originally went down she was above the waterline but time has taken its toll and she is now broken up and lying beneath the waves. Owing to the shallow depth she is largely a snorkel site and even then there is not a great deal to see. There can be strong currents which can pull one away from the main wreck site, and much of the wreckage is on the far side of the reef. This is an ancient wreck site, in hostile waters, and so is not for the inexperienced diver.

The **Cali**, also called the 'Rice Ship', was lost off George Town harbour in January 1948. She was a steel Colombian motor vessel launched in August 1900 from a British shipyard. She sailed under four

Martha Watkins Gilkes exploring the wreck of the *Balboa* (Richard McCrea)

(previous spread) Divers on the bicycle on the wreck of the *Oro Verde* different names and four different flags in her day. From 1900 to 1927 she sailed as the *Hawaii* and although American owned, was under a Chilean flag until 1902, as foreign-built vessels could not fly the US flag. From 1926 until 1933 she was the *Ethel M. Stering* and sailed under an American flag. From 1933 to 1946 she sailed under a Mexican flag as the *Hidalgo* and in 1946 she became the *Cali* under a Colombian flag. She sailed from Guayaquil, Ecuador, on 9 January 1948 but developed leaks in bad weather and had to head for the nearest port, which was Grand Cayman. She was eventually abandoned and even set on fire. She lay in shallow water for some time and was deemed a shipping hazard. In 1957 (along with the *Balboa*) she was blown up by the British Corps of Engineers.

The **Arbutus** is an ancient wooden wreck south of the *Cali*. The structure is long gone, with only ballast stones remaining. Occasionally artefacts are located but cannot be taken from the site.

**Wanderer IX** has little to attest to its existence. All that remains is a lead keel in 6 ft of water on the reef off Colliers. This vessel sank in October 1964, according to *An Adventurer's Guide to the Unspoiled Cayman Islands* by George Hudson.

The schooner **Geneva Kathleen** sank in 1930. The site has been under non-intrusive archaeological research from Ball State University. Oral histories have been taken with the hope of mounting an exhibition and publishing the findings.

There is one particularly fascinating story about the wrecks in the Cayman waters. The **Ten Sail Wreck** has been well documented, and divers interested in historical wrecks can find much research by Dr Margaret E. Leshikar-Denton, archaeologist at the Cayman Islands National Museum. These unfortunate ten sailing ships fell upon great misfortune in February 1794. The HMS *Convert* was a newly commissioned Royal Navy frigate under the command of Captain John Lawford. A convoy of merchantmen, laden with sugar and rum from the islands, was to be escorted by the *Convert* and was en route to England from Jamaica during the French Revolutionary wars. According to Dr Leshikar-Denton, at the beginning of the journey the fleet was delayed by a leaky merchant ship. The *Convert*'s officers were unable to sight Grand Cayman before the sun set on the second day of the voyage. Around midnight the watch recommended to the captain that the course be changed; he reckoned the fleet was west and southward of Grand Cayman. Some of the merchantmen had disobeyed

*(below and opposite)*
**The wreck of the Russian ship MV** ***Captain Keith Tibbetts*** *(Wayne Hasson)*

**The *Doc Poulson***
(*Wayne Hasson*)

orders and sailed ahead of the naval escort; they were wrecked on the windward reefs of Grand Cayman. One of these ships fired a warning shot but when Captain Lawford tried to change course another merchantman crashed into the *Convert*'s bow. Dawn revealed all nine merchantmen and the HMS *Convert* aground. The inhabitants of Grand Cayman helped rescue survivors but there were limited provisions and supplies on the island and Captain Lawford arranged for most of her crew to be taken onboard other ships of the fleet to return to England.

The ships were all heavily salvaged by the owners and also by Caymanians. In modern times, in a study supported in part by a Texas A & M fellowship and the National Museum, interesting remains have been located. These include cannons, fragments of glass and ceramics, and anchors. Much has been written about these ships. In 1994 the Cayman Island government created a park at East End which provides a view to the reef where the tragedy occurred. This move was an effort to acknowledge the importance of the historical wrecks of the islands.

## Cayman Brac

The first-class wreck already mentioned, the *Captain Keith Tibbetts*, is located at Cayman Brac. Others include the *Cayman Mariner*, the *Kissimee* and the *Buccaneer*. The 60 ft **Kissimee** is an iron tug and lies inverted at 45–66 ft. She was deliberately sunk in 1982. She is located at the north end of Stake Bay not far from the *Captain Keith Tibbetts*.

The 65 ft **Cayman Mariner** lies upright near East Chutes drop-off. This was an aluminum boat sunk in 1986. The **Buccaneer** is similarly sited to *Kissimee*, at the north end of Stake Bay in 45–66 ft of water.

The **Captain Keith Tibbetts**, named in honour of a deceased legendary sea captain from Cayman Brac, was formerly a Russian destroyer. She was known as No. 356 and was sunk in September 1996 in the waters off Cayman Brac. She has been dubbed the only divable Russian warship in the western world. Marine environmentalist Jean-Michel Cousteau actually rode her to the bottom of the sea as she was sunk, during filming for a documentary entitled *Destroyer for Peace*. The name 'Destroyer for Peace' refers to the symbolism of this former killing machine being the basis for new life, as marine growth attaches to her and lives in and around her.

The story of how this wreck came to rest on the bottom of the sea off Cayman Brac is a long one. No. 356 was first spotted in January 1996 tied up along a pier in a Cuban navy base. Wayne Hasson, part owner of the *Aggressor* fleet of live-aboard dive boats, was with the *Cayman Aggressor* in Cuba while she was in dry dock and could see No. 356 nearby. He learned she was going to be scrapped. She was not in a good condition and was being used to supply spare parts for two other similar destroyers. Wayne had a vision that this ship could be a wonderful shipwreck for the Cayman Islands. He returned to the Caymans and through his initiative the Ministry of the Environment and Tourism became interested in the project. Wayne continued to pursue the project and made flights back and forth in its pursuit. In fact, on one ill fated trip he crashed (and lost) his private aeroplane, and is fortunate to have survived. Serious negotiations were held with the Cuban government and after a year $219,750 US was paid to purchase No. 356. The Cayman government and SITA (Sister Island Tourism Association) purchased the ship from the Russian Embassy. An additional $10,000 was paid for the guns to be left in place. Other costs, according to Hasson, included $48,000 to the cleaning company to make the ship ready to sink, $17,000 to tow it from Cuba to Cayman Brac, and $9000 to anchor and sink her. This made the grand total for this unique wreck site $303,750.

Before this massive ship could be sunk the port authority measured the vessel and determined that it was too tall; they required the mast that held the radar to be cut down. In September 1997 when No. 356 arrived from Cuba at Cayman, many Caymanians came aboard and removed small pieces of the ship. Today nearly every home in Cayman Brac and even some on nearby Little Cayman have a piece of the ship displayed. According to Wayne Hasson this was not a bad thing as the removal of small items did not damage the ship and gave the Caymanians a sense of pride in their local wreck.

There is an interesting aside to the sinking of the *Captain Keith Tibbetts*: a retired Russian officer who had served aboard No. 356 traced her history and learned that she had been purchased to sink as an artificial reef in Cayman Brac. When he was in the USA the officer sought out Wayne Hasson at the Diving Equipment Manufacturers' Association Show and presented him with some of the pins from his personal uniform he had worn aboard No. 356 years before.

The wreck now lies at peace on a slope from 50 to 80 ft deep on the bottom 900 yards off the north shore of Cayman Brac. She offers three decks to swim through and the missile launcher; the machine gun turrets, deck cannons and living quarters are all available for exploration. The ship was home for 11 officers and 99 enlisted men. She had two diesel and turbine engines. This great ship will give pleasure to wreck divers for years to come, thanks to Wayne Hasson's vision.

On the south shore of Cayman Brac the **Prince Frederick** wreck is located off Hawksbill Bay. This wooden hulled, twin masted schooner is 110 ft long and lies from 20 to 50 ft deep. She was powered by steam and is thought to have sunk in the late 1800s although this is not definite. There is much scrap metal lying around the reef including the windlass, anchor and chains, cast iron masts and copper nails.

## Little Cayman

The 120 ft **Soto Trader** lies in the waters on the south side of Little Cayman. She was a steel hulled cargo ship, a major supplier of cargo for Little Cayman. She caught fire while transferring fuel and sank in April 1975. She lies in 60 ft of water with plenty of growth on her. Two jeep chassis are still to be found in her hold.

The wrecks of the Cayman Islands are many and varied in size, depth, age and diving interest – there is something for everyone. Further information can be found in *The Dive Sites of the Cayman Islands* by Lawson Wood (New Holland Publishers).

# Dominica

1. *Barge*
2. *Canefield Tug*
3. *Douwe-S*
4. *Debbie-Flo*
5. *Sonja*
6. *Champagne Wrecks*

Wreck diving does not feature prominently on Dominica; it does not need to – the wall and reef dives are so spectacular that most divers can't get enough diving on these sites. However, there are a few known divable wreck sites, at least two of which have been put down intentionally to provide choices for the wreck diver. In addition, Dominica's past history of ancient wrecks is rich and exciting and the stories of ships that are rumoured to have sunk around the island (but have never been located) will captivate even those who are blasé about wrecks. Major hurricanes struck Dominica in 1766, 1769, 1772, 1776, 1780, 1787, 1792 and 1813 and many ships were lost in them. Lloyds of London list over 65 vessels lost off Roseau, the capital.

Of the known divable wrecks mentioned below, only three are really worth diving, but they are all described because their stories are of historical interest.

The **Barge**, a shallow wreck lying upside down in only 40 ft, is seldom dived, but is sometimes used as a night dive because of the many basket starfish attached to her structure. These magnificent invertebrates only open their delicate tendrils after dark, and although they are found on the reefs of Dominica also, they are a special attraction here. Numerous rope sponges, sea plums and yellow tube sponges are also growing on the structure.

**Divers inside the *Canefield Tug***

The ***Canefield Tug***, a 55 ft tug built in 1918, lies in 90 ft of water on a silty bottom. There is no reef life near her, so diving on the site is limited to exploring the wreck itself. The location also makes this site difficult. She sits near the mouth of the Canefield River and often run-off from the mountains down the river causes sediment to be suspended in the first 40–60 ft of the sea. This makes for poor visibility while descending on the site. There is also a stone crushing plant nearby which sometimes causes sediment in the water.

The *Canefield Tug* belonged to the Dominica Mining Company and was used for about five years to tow a barge from Dominica to the US Virgin Islands and Puerto Rico to transport sand and pumice stone mined in Dominica. She was washed ashore by Hurricane David in 1979, and some of her internal works were sold at this time. She was refloated, but within a short time she sank at anchor and sits in the very spot where she went down.

She is home for schools of reef fish and features wire coral and hydroids. Black margate and large barracuda, jacks and mackerel also cruise around the site. Descents are often murky in the first 20 ft because of suspended particles in the water, but the visibility usually clears below this.

One of two intentionally sunken wreck sites, put down as a diving site in July 1990, is the **Douwe-S**, located at Anse Bateau on a sandy slope 50–73 ft deep. She takes her name from her original owner, Mr S. Douwe from Holland. Mr Douwe had commissioned the building of the 255 ton ship, which had a 22 ft wide beam and was 117 ft long, in 1936.

Fifty years later she was washed ashore by a freak storm which hit Dominica in November 1987. Just a few years prior to this, while she was still a working ship, Mr Douwe's son traced her to the island of Dominica and requested a visit to the ship; the owner happily agreed.

In 1972 the *Douwe-S* came to the West Indies from Holland, having been bought by Mr Clarke of Barbados. It took Mr Clarke and his crew 22 days to bring her across the Atlantic, to St Vincent where she was registered. She remained a Vincencian registered ship until her demise.

**Diver Tony Gilkes gazes through a porthole of the *Douwe-S***

She plied the waters between Barbados and Trinidad until 1977 when Mr Clarke sold her to Dominican Lionel Pinard. She changed her course to travel between St Lucia, Dominica and Guadeloupe. Once a month she carried Heineken beer, manufactured in St Lucia, to Dominica. The other three weeks of the month she ran a course between the islands, carrying fresh produce.

Before the tragic fatal storm which led to her sinking, she had been a lucky lady in her prior encounters with hurricanes and storms in the Caribbean. In August 1979 she had escaped the devastating Hurricane David, which hit Dominica with the full impact of winds of 150 miles per hour. Her owner Mr Lionel Pinard wisely took her away from Dominican waters to the safety of St Lucia. Upon returning to the island four days later, he learned of yet another hurricane approaching and for several days the *Douwe-S* rode out the bad weather at sea. She returned to the island unscarred, but with a worn-out crew of seven who had battled the elements of nature through two storms. For six months after Hurricane David the *Douwe-S* did charity work, supplying the island with cement and material for galvanised roofing from nearby islands, in order to help the rebuilding after the storm.

She was not to remain so lucky in her next encounter with a hurricane. In November 1987 Dominica was hit by a hurricane which took many by surprise, producing 6 ft swells and winds out of the southwest. The winds raged for five days and when they finally subsided, the *Douwe-S* was firmly aground in Woodbridge Bay. She was not the only ship to suffer. In the Roseau area, four ships were lost, and in Portsmouth on the northern end of the island, five ships were

destroyed. By this time her owner, who had been her captain until 1981, had purchased a second ship, which he was commanding at the time of the storm, so he was not onboard to help secure her.

The *Douwe-S* sat in the bay like a mighty reminder of the wrath of nature, from 1985 until 1990, when the owner turned her over to the government and advised them he could do nothing with her. She was actually in the way of the expansion of the deep water harbour so the

**Peter Benchley and Dominican diver Derek Perryman explore wreckage off Dominica**

government was forced to take a decision as to her fate. Because of her large size and the fact that she was firmly aground, she was not easy to move. After discussions with the dive shops of the island, the fisheries division made a decision to sink her as a diving site. She was cut into three parts: the bow, the mid-section and the stern. This made it easier to pull her off the shoreline.

Dominica is the last home of the Carib Indians in the Caribbean

The **Debbie Flo**, lying in 80–90 ft, is actually tied to the *Douwe-S* and you can follow the line from one wreck to the other. She was built between 1968 and 1972 in St Augusta, Florida. This wooden hulled boat was 72 ft long, 21 ft wide and drew 6 ft.

The owner was having maintenance problems because of her wooden hull and wanted to dispose of her. She was in the main port of the island being stripped to be sunk in deep water when Dive Dominica, the longest established diving shop on the island, purchased her for $1000 EC in 1993. On the day of sinking she was towed to her location by *Yan*, the dive boat of Dive Dominca, under Derek Perryman, and tied to the *Douwe-S*. Lionel Pinard, owner of the *Douwe-S*, was holding her off with another boat. Her seacocks were seized shut, so holes had to be punched in her side to allow her slowly to take on water and sink to her present location.

The **Sonja** is a steel hulled 106 ft freighter, built in 1899 in Holland. She sank in 1995 and lies just north of the *Canefield Tug* off Donkey Beach, Canefield.

Near a well known diving site, 'Champagne', at the west end of the island, are remains of three wrecks: a wooden shrimp boat, a steel inner island fighter and a very ancient wreck, together known as the **Champagne Wrecks**.

Hurricane Luis uncovered the ancient site, which is possibly 250 to 300 years old. Some copper sheathing on the site gives indications that it is a British ship. Three cannon lie fused together, and some old planking and the odd nail can be seen in only 18 ft of water.

On the north end of the island, seldom dived, there are wreck sites scattered around the coastline. At the entrance to Tocukary Bay there are remains from around 1880 of a site, but the exact location is unknown.

On Dominica wall and reef diving tend to overshadow wreck diving and dive shops do not actively promote wreck exploration, but for the enthusiast there are several sites on offer.

# Grenada

In the wreck diving world, Grenada's claim to fame is as home to probably the largest and most famous wreck of the Caribbean: the 584 ft *Bianca C*, sometimes called the *Titanic* or the *Andrea Dora* of the Caribbean. There are few divable wrecks that compare with this massive structure.

As on most of the islands, many of the wrecks with a known history are modern day wrecks; however, there are records of ancient sites. Some of these are considered 'treasure wrecks'. The Portuguese merchantman *Armida* was lost in 1805, carrying valuable cargo. Accounts indicate that most was recovered. However on 22 January 1816 the richly laden Spanish merchantman *Virgen del Rosario* was wrecked off Point Saline and only a small part of her cargo was rescued! Local divers on the island tell of finding cannon in this area, possibly from the *Virgen del Rosario*.

The modern wrecks date from 1900 to the present, with some having been sunk as diving sites, and others the result of tragic losses at sea.

One of the intentionally sunk wrecks, and one of the most popular for an easy wreck dive, is the **Buccaneer**, put down in 1977. She was a 42 ft two masted, steel hulled sloop. She lies on her starboard side in

Molinière Bay. She was owned by a Mr Campbell, who operated her as a charter yacht between Grenada and Martinique. The steel hull had developed holes and she was actually taking on water and slowly sinking in the marina owned by Grenada Yacht Services (GYS).

The port of Grenada

These were the pioneer days of diving, when the reefs were still unexplored in Grenada and the intentional sinking of wrecks had not yet become popular; there was only one dive shop on the island, owned by an American, Leroy French. French, along with his young divemaster, Grenadian Mosden Cumberbatch, knew that the *Buccaneer* would make a great diving site and the owner gladly donated her to the cause. French left Grenada many years ago, but Mosden, still on the island and very active in the watersports world, kindly related details of the sinking. The *Buccaneer* had to be refloated, using barrels, and pumped out before she could be towed from GYS. *Sanddollar*, French's dive boat, with the help of *Gambia*, a deep sea fishing boat, towed her to her location. She was positioned in the planned place of sinking and as she slowly sank to the bottom, Mosden and diver Fabian, equipped with dive gear, actually rode her to the seabed, making this the first dive on her. Within two days tourist divers were taken back to the site. She now rests in 75 ft near Molinière Reef.

Although not a difficult dive, there can be current on the site. The *Buccaneer* is now covered in soft corals and hydroids and offers some excellent photographic opportunities. There is also rare black coral growing on the wreck

The prop was still attached until around 1984, and made a good shot for photographers; however, one day Mosden found that careless visiting divers had sawn off the prop, presumably to take home as a souvenir or perhaps to sell for a few dollars. They had been unsuccessful in raising the prop from the seabed; otherwise it would have been taken off the island (technically stolen, according to Grenadian law).

In addition to the structure itself, the site offers the experience of observing a school of garden eels gently swaying in the sand, and a yellow headed jawfish is always nearby in his permanent burrow, popping up to nibble at a passing bit of plankton. In the past there was a resident sea horse clinging to a nearby gorgonia; most likely he is still there, as they seldom move home. A nice ending to the dive is the exploration of the shallow Molinière Reef, which ascends to 15 ft. Coral encrusted lava flows gently tumble down the sand slope, forming channels through which divers can ascend. These lava flows attest to the days of volcanic activity on the island.

The most famous wreck of Grenada, the **Bianca C**, will be eternally remembered not just by divers, but throughout Grenada. One might wonder what makes the *Bianca C* so unique and special. To start with, her size is awesome. For the British, she would equal nine cricket pitches in length; for Americans, two football fields would barely hold her! Few divable shipwrecks are so large. Also, her story is well documented, adding to the romance and interest of the dive; it is not always easy to find out the background of a wreck. Everything that was onboard the ship, except the passengers and crew, went down with her. Although she is not a beginner's dive, she offers many levels of diving for those with good experience, especially if accompanied by an expert dive guide. She can be dived at under 100 ft by staying above the

**Smoke billows from the stricken Bianca C**

structure, or she can be seriously penetrated and explored by very experienced wreck divers.

While the story of the cruise ship *Bianca C* was known throughout the island, and had been published locally and regionally, she had not attracted international press attention except at the time of her sinking. In 1989, 28 years after the sinking, the US *Forbes Magazine* published a feature on her. Cumberbatch, mentioned above as one of the pioneers in the development of diving on the island, was instrumental in this effort. His business, HMC Dive Center, invited *Forbes* writer Pat Canova and editor Bill Falligan to the island to tell the story of the *Bianca C*. The article was reprinted in 1981 in *Greetings*, the Grenada tourist publication. Since that time much has been written about the ship, some of it inaccurate.

A large bronze statue of Jesus Christ, entitled 'Christ of the Deep' stands inside the deep water harbour in St John's, to her memory. The statue, presented by the Italian Costa Line, owners of the cruise ship, is also in honour of the people of Grenada for the role they played in this tragedy. Originally the statue was located at the entrance to the St George's harbour, but was not easily visible in this location. A decision was made to relocate the statue to the present site.

The nightmare of *Bianca C*'s final days began in the early morning hours of 22 October 1961. The ship was on an exotic Caribbean cruise,

'Christ of the Deep', the statue in honour of the bravery of the Grenadian people during the accident involving the *Bianca C*, in its original location in St George's

**Massive black coral trees grow on the *Bianca C***

with the Spice Island as her last port of call. She was preparing to return to her home port when an explosion in the engine room caused a fire that quickly spread. Her 400 passengers and 200 crew, as well as the people of Grenada, were awakened in the early hours by the startling alarm of tragedy. Miraculously, the only lives lost were those of two crew members who were killed in the fire. The Grenadian people rushed to the rescue of the passengers in anything that would stay afloat, taking them into their homes. The *Bianca C* lay burning just outside St George's harbour for two days, while distress calls went out all through the Caribbean. There was great concern that she would sink on site and block the entrance to the harbour.

The frigate HMS *Londonderry* was two days away and came to the rescue when the distress call was sounded. Plans to beach her on a shallow reef, so that whatever did remain could be salvaged, were not to be realised. The towline pulled apart and she floundered about, slowly sinking beneath the waves, the water literally hissing and boiling around her, on 24 October 1961.

She lies off Point Saline on the southwest corner of the island, having come to rest on her starboard side in 160 ft of water. The port side is slightly more shallow, in 150 ft. The bow has broken away and the upper decks and the swimming pool have begun to cave in under the weight and stress. The structure is covered in massive black coral trees and attracts pelagic marine life such as big groupers, jewfish, large barracuda, horse-eye and black jacks. More gentle marine life such as queen angels are also seen on the site. French angelfish have taken up residence and are usually seen on every dive.

Much still remains on the ship, although the props were salvaged. Visiting divers have also removed many mementoes of her grand days, including the ship's bell and much of the china and cutlery, which used to be seen by divers as they swam through the superstructure. A photograph of the bell is pictured in the book *Tropical Shipwrecks* by Daniel and Denise Berg. It shows two of the divers from Long Island, New York, who recovered the bell, Hank Garvin and Chris Dillon; the third diver who took part, Rick Schwarz, took the photograph. They feel they broke no law in removing the bell and other artefacts from the *Bianca C*, and taking them to the USA; in fact they feel they 'saved the artefacts from destruction'. However, to the people of Grenada, who view the *Bianca C* as a monument, this was an atrocious violation. In an interview held in Grenada Mr Andrew Bierzynsky, then president of the Grenada National Trust, expressed great concern over the removal of the bell from island. Those who value history on Grenada hope that in time a proper museum will be built to tell the story of the *Bianca C* in more detail (there is a small one at present which houses some of the artefacts). Perhaps the bell could one day be returned to the people of Grenada for their new museum.

The *Bianca C* is not a beginner's dive. It should only be dived with one of the local dive operators, who are experienced in diving the site. There can be strong currents, which make the descent and ascent difficult; sometimes descent is only made hand over hand by rope. In strong currents decompression stops, and hanging on the anchor rope can be challenging. Photographers with cumbersome camera equipment have to be especially careful, although the site offers some spectacular photographic possibilities. However, for the experienced diver under the guidance of a good local dive shop, and especially the wreck diver, the site is a must. The best part of the wreck for exploration is from the smokestack back to the stern section, as the open superstructure and tremendous amount of growth add to the excitement of the dive.

For some years, the *Carla C*, an exact sister ship to the *Bianca C*, called on Grenada, bringing tourists to enjoy the Spice Island and providing a reminder of the *Bianca C*.

On the Atlantic side of the island lies the SS **Orinoco**, a steam and sail powered vessel which sank in 1990 off La Sagesse Point. The story goes that the local custom (which is still practised) of lighting candles on the graves of dead relatives on All Souls Night caused the *Orinoco* helmsman mistakenly to identify the hundreds of flickering lights in the graveyard as the lights of St George's, the capital. Turning towards the candle lights, he rammed St David's Point at full speed.

The wreck sits in 9–30 ft of water and appears to be about 120 ft long. The steel masts lie to the side, the large boiler sits at a tilt and the ship is broken into pieces, scattered about the reef. The propeller is still attached and the ship's bell is to be found at the Grenada prison. There are often strong currents around the wreck and large schools of barracuda are found. Underwater exploration was done (on this and other sites) in 1983 by the Foundation for Field Research out of San Diego, California, headed by Tom Banks. This group was a non-profit making organisation which used volunteer divers willing to contribute a tax deductible share of the project's costs and labour. This expedition had a sad ending for Grenada. Mr Andrew Bierzynski confirmed that not only did the Foundation fail to provide the promised documentation on the sites they researched, but they removed numerous artefacts from the island, claiming they would be returned after 'conservation'. Interviews with prominent Grenadians also confirmed that there were outstanding debts owed to a number of local people. All too often this scenario occurs on other islands as well, and trusting nationals believe the grandiose schemes put forward by foreigners. Sadly, this has resulted in those who are legitimate and can offer some help in wreck exploration, and documentation and artefact recovery for museums and historical societies, being viewed as potential exploiters.

Several boats have been sunk as a result of being involved in legal battles over various illicit activities – drug running, smuggling illegal goods, and so on. The **Don Cesard**, which sank in 1995, operated as a drug runner. She was caught and confiscated by the Grenada coastguard and sat at anchor for some time. She was taking on water and began to sink, however, and so the coastguard towed her to her present location and allowed her to sink in 90 ft of water. She now lies near Molinière Reef and the *Buccaneer* wreck.

The 120 ft **Veronica L** (originally named the *Illiation*) and the 160 ft **Ginny S** were Grenadian owned steel cargo ships from Holland. They lie within 50 yards of each other just outside St George's harbour in only 40 ft of water. They plied the waters all over the Caribbean, carrying whatever cargo they could obtain. Both were impounded for illegal shipping and both were left for so long while the conflict was being debated that they sank as a result of neglect.

*Three Wrecks*, named by the diving community, is actually three-quarters of a large cargo vessel, the *Unity Courier*. She was also being held on suspicion of illegal shipping, and so had been impounded by the government. The *Unity Courier* sank originally inside St George's harbour. She was a navigational hazard to the main harbour of the island, so the government had her cut up and moved. Her 'fourth quarter', now called **Quarter Wreck**, was accidentally dropped in shallow water (25–35 ft) off Grand Anse Reef, instead of being placed with the rest of the structure. This is considered another wreck site, although it is actually part of the *Unity Courier*.

*Three Wrecks* (*Unity Courier*) lies in 40 ft of water off Quarantine Point (the location of the old leper colony on the island). There can be strong currents in this area and speedboats often operate here, so great care is required when diving on this site.

*Fiona*, approximately 100 ft long, was a St Vincent owned cement boat that is now off L'Anse aux Epines in only 15 ft of water. She hit the rocks and put out an SOS, but by the time anyone went to her aid she was sinking. There are usually strong currents running around her and many barracuda  inhabit the wreck.

Divers only discovered the **Atlantic Wreck**, so called because of her location on the Atlantic side of the island, in early August 1998. The photographs here are the earliest shots of her underwater. Little is known about the site. The wreck appears to be a fishing boat, approximately 50 ft long and lying upright on a flat coral rubble bed in 80 ft

**Nurse sharks and diver on the *Atlantic Wreck***

of water. Four large nurse sharks are obviously very much at home around the site and were a bit perturbed about divers invading their space. Gentle French angelfish are also on the site and a mass of grunt cover the deck. A large turtle carcass lies in the bow, as though an old turtle gave up the ghost gracefully on the deck. A local lobster fisherman shared the site with the diving community, opening up another exciting diving wreck.

There is a site off Glover Island that was created as part of the clean-up effort following the military intervention of 1979. It is a mix of military machinery and old jeeps that were destroyed during the action. Although not a regular dive site, like anything put down on the seabed it will attract coral growth and marine life. In time, the tragedy of the events surrounding the intervention will be forgotten as these former artefacts of war become artificial reefs and enhance the marine environment.

The wrecks mentioned here are not all the wrecks of Grenada – there is not room to cover every one in detail. But certainly for the serious wreck diver, if the only wreck on Grenada were the *Bianca C*, she alone would merit a diving holiday to Grenada, as she is one of a kind!

# St Kitts and Nevis

St Kitts and Nevis, like most of the Caribbean islands, are known to have been home to many ancient shipwrecks. According to Robert Marx's book, *Shipwrecks of the Western Hemisphere* (McKay & Co., NY, 1975), some 390 ships were lost around these waters between 1492 and 1825. These were from many nations, including Britain, Spain, the Netherlands and America. Many were warships and merchant ships, but there were some pirate ships also, as has been confirmed in recent years when hurricanes have uncovered some interesting sites; one is called the *Pirate Wreck*.

The earliest wrecks around St Kitts discussed by Marx are from 1629 when the Spanish attacked the French and English, and four ships were sunk in the harbour. In 1642, a hurricane sank 23 English ships and in 1733, in a June hurricane, 12 ships went down at Basseterre. The list continues, with most of the wrecks being from hurricanes or storms, although a number are noted as having gone down in battles. For the history enthusiast and the serious wreck researcher, the stories of these undiscovered wrecks are gripping.

**Brimstone Hill Fortress**

St Kitts is also home to the historic Brimstone Hill Fortress, termed the 'Gibraltar of the West Indies'. This 38 acre fortress is one of the largest pre-twentieth-century fortifications in the world. In 1736 the fort boasted at least 49 cannon. While the English were her main occupants, the French successfully invaded in 1782. Where there are forts, especially of the magnitude of Brimstone Hill, there are ships. And where there are ships, there are shipwrecks. So it stands to reason that a number of the ancient wrecks said to be in the waters around St Kitts would have an association with the fortress. There has never been any serious excavation done on ancient shipwrecks in St Kitts, but local divers describe the 'bumps' of massive coral heads that grow over obvious old wrecks. The shapes are not like normal coral reef; often at one end of the 'bump' of coral an anchor chain can be observed or sometimes timbers. There are also a number of modern day wrecks on St Kitts, providing the diver with a choice of almost more wreck sites than one can dive in a reasonable time.

While nearby Nevis does not offer any modern shipwrecks, there are records of many ancient wrecks, and this is also the location of James Town. For the archaeologically minded diver, James Town, the first settlement on the island, is particularly exciting. James Town was located on the west coast and while most of the time there is nothing to see of it, when the sands shift, especially after storms, structures have been sighted. It is accepted that James Town lies below the sea and it is believed that this port town literally slipped below the waves as a result of a tidal wave or an earthquake. Some documents record this as taking place on 30 April 1680, while others put forward a date in 1860. Marx states that this dramatic event took place on 6 April 1690. He also mentions that in 1961, during an exploratory dive on the site, he located a number of buildings protruding above the seabed and 20 huge cannon. Local fishermen and scuba divers claim that they have heard the church bells tolling in the area. One local diver confirmed he had seen stone remains. Marine salvage expert and treasure hunter Teddy Tucker of Bermuda said that many years ago he saw some remains of the town. The exact location is a mystery, but perhaps one day a lucky diver will chance upon some definite evidence that will help to clarify the mystery shrouding this ghost town.

The largest shipwreck around the waters of St Kitts, listed among the 20 best wrecks of the Caribbean by *Skin Diver* magazine, is the 144 ft **River Taw**. She started her life in the UK and was later brought to the Caribbean.

The wreck of the *River Taw*, covered with soft corals and marine growth

Her purchase was an innovative move. Until this time most of the transportation between the islands was done by small, locally built, wooden boats. To bring a large metal hulled cargo ship out to the islands, although soon to become a more common practice, was at this time a first and showed considerable recourcefulness on the part of her new owners. It was such a 'speculative' move that long-time St Kitts shipping agent, Mr Al Barker, recalled this particular proposal being discussed at the St Kitts Chamber of Commerce prior to the purchase of the *River Taw*. Her new Caribbean crew, with the help of a British pilot, undertook her Atlantic crossing. After her arrival in St Kitts, Captain Ralph Saunders took command.

For a number of years the *River Taw* carried cargo from Barbados to St Kitts and to Puerto Rico. In addition, she had the contract with the St Kitts government to transport flour from St Vincent on a regular basis. In the early 1970s, during a hurricane, she dragged her anchor and was washed ashore; she actually sat on top of the pier in Basseterre harbour. She was eventually pulled off into deeper water, partly under her own power and partly with the help of several small vessels, where she sat at anchor for eight months. During that time, Kittian diver Kenneth Samuel was hired to plug six 2 inch holes on her port side with wooden plugs, which stabilised her for approximately one year until the plugs rotted. He was then hired to replug the holes and again she was stabilised. However, the harbourmaster felt the *River Taw* was a hazard and had her moved from her anchorage off Basseterre to Frigate Bay, where she sat for approximately another year. The plugs were again rotting, and this time the *River Taw* did not receive the attention she needed. In time, she took on water and by 1979 she had slowly sunk to her final resting place.

She now lies in 47 ft of water in Frigate Bay. For some years her prop was still attached, but in recent years it has mysteriously disappeared. In 1989, during Hurricane Hugo, she was badly damaged and the once

French angelfish inhabit the interior of the wreck of the *River Taw*

easily penetrable wreck was broken into two pieces. During the 1995 hurricane season, Hurricane Marilyn and then Hurricane Luis actually moved the two pieces of the wreckage; the stern section was not only shifted but completely turned through 180°. During the early years of her life underwater, the stern was lying with its port side in the sand. As a result the starboard side developed a lush marine growth of gorgonians and soft corals. Large French angelfish and schools of blackbar soldierfish filled the interior. However in September 1995, not only was she moved some 150 ft from her original location; she was turned upright. This has exposed the entire upper interior, so it is hoped the growth will now spread.

In October 1992, to enhance the marine life in the area, Kenneth Samuel, owner of the longest established dive shop on the island, placed nine car bodies around the site about 50 ft apart. For some time this attracted fish life and added to the dive. However, the hurricanes mentioned above have now moved most of the car bodies.

Another well known dive site on the island is the 120 ft **Talata**, lying in Potato Bay. It appears there was a dispute between the Development Bank of St Kitts and the owners of the ship, and the bank seized the boat. During this time it sat at anchor for six to seven months with a watchman aboard. However, one of the seacocks was leaking and for some time the vessel was pumped out to prevent sinking. Eventually she was taking on too much water and the coast guard had to rescue the watchman as *Talata* was sinking. She went to the bottom in 1985. This site is a spectacular night dive and divers are almost guaranteed to see turtles. The 60 ft dive affords diverse masses of fish life. Three volcanic vents associated with the volcanic part of the island add interest to the site. One vent is about 50 ft from the bow on the port side; another is about 80 ft from the stern, also on the port side; the third vent has now stopped producing hot water. It appears that these warm water vents attract the numerous turtles usually seen on the site.

The Island Dredging Company has contributed to the wrecks of St Kitts, including the *Brimstone Shallows* site, *Scrap* and the *Corinthia*.

**Brimstone Shallows** off Fort Thomas is an assortment of equipment and scrap items that were of no use on land. These metal pieces were placed on a sandy bottom and are becoming a refuge for marine life. In time coral will grow and cover the area.

Hurricane Luis in September 1995 was responsible for the wreckage of the barge handling tugboat *Corinthia* and the two massive 270 ft barges, the *Stephanie M* and *Recovery*. In order to remove these large barges from the shoreline, they were cut into large pieces and sunk in October 1995. They now make up a dive site dubbed **Scrap**, located outside Frigate Bay. This 70 ft dive consists of a variety of scrap wreck pieces and the two large barges, which were also part of the St Kitts port project. The site has become home for invertebrate marine life and many lobsters have found safe shelter under the large sheets of metal.

**The wreck of the Corinthia**          The **Corinthia** was built in Louisiana and was bought by the Island Dredging Company of Jamaica around 1978. Named after a member of the family who owns the company, she was a single screw tug, 86 ft long and 22 ft wide, with a twin inline diesel engine. *Corinthia* served most of her time in Jamaica as a heavy-duty tug and had only a short life in St Kitts. The Island Dredging Company came to the island in 1994 to help build the new St Kitts port for cruise ship arrivals. *Corinthia* arrived in February 1995, to begin her time as an important tug in the construction work. On 4 September 1995, along with a number of other vessels belonging to Island Dredging, the *Corinthia* was thought to be safely moored on a hurricane mooring off Basseterre, prepared to ride out the onslaught of Hurricane Luis. No one bargained for the raging seas that would be part of this devastating storm. Some 36 hours later the *Corinthia* lay broken and bashed against the rocks south of Friars Bay. Her sister barge, the 65 ft *Lewis M*, was washed up on Bay Road, but being smaller and not as badly damaged, was salvageable. The *Corinthia* was an old girl; because of the extensive damage it was determined that she had come to the end of her useful days. During her hard working life she had sunk and been raised twice before; the third accident was the final straw. Rather than being scrapped or cut to pieces, she met a graceful end. After the decision had been made to sink her, the Island Dredging Company put temporary marine epoxy patches on her in order to refloat her. On 23 October 1995 she was towed to her final resting place, not far from the site where another sister barge, the 65 ft *Lugger*, was washed ashore. The patches were then removed and after some two hours of taking on water she gently sank to the sandy seabed in 70 ft of water, near Broad Bar Reef. She is completely intact and proudly sitting perfectly upright, surrounded by marine life. Adventurous divers can now visit *Corinthia*, to photograph and appreciate her. Life is slowly growing and in time she will undergo a sea change into a thing of beauty, with marine life finding safe shelter in her structure. This is a fitting ending for a grand old girl who served her time well for over 20 years in the Caribbean waters.

White House Bay on the Atlantic side of St Kitts is the site of two wrecks, both of which can easily be snorkelled over. The **Tugboat** lies in only 20 ft of water. Her origin is not certain, but she was probably used at a time when salt was collected in this area.

At the opposite end of White House Bay, Hurricane Luis uncovered an eighteeth-century wreck termed the *Pirate Wreck* in 1995. This site lies in only 6–8 ft of water, and the main evidence of the ship's existence is some rotting wooden timbers and six iron cannon. There have been other small artefacts discovered around the site.

The **Brassball Wreck** is another site that can be snorkelled over, as she lies in only 20–25 ft of water on a sandy bottom. She was a small wooden boat bringing supplies for the sugar factory, and sank around 1940. She lies about a quarter of a mile off Fort Point, where the Fort Thomas Hotel is located. She is covered in marine growth, and is home to masses of small fish and invertebrate life. In fact, Kenneth Samuel estimates that there are about two hundred types of invertebrate life on the site.

Two ferryboats have sunk off St Kitts. *La Amigo*, an 80–90 ft ferry built in the UK, ran aground in Hurricane Hugo in 1989 and lay on land owned by the government treasury for over five years. Around 1991, the government hired a US salvage team to pull her off and sink her less than a mile from the wreck of the *Talata*. She now lies in 60 ft of water off Fort Thomas Hotel.

The tragic sinking of MV *Christina* on 1 August 1970 is still remembered with much sadness by local people, as so many family and loved ones were lost, on a scheduled voyage between St Kitts and Nevis. Such is the strength of local feeling that MV *Christina* is not promoted as a diving wreck. In fact, several of the dive shops refuse to take divers on this site and are outraged when other dive operators allow visitors to dive there. It is felt that the MV *Christina* should be viewed as a memorial, much like the ships of Turk Lagoon in the Pacific. I include her here, among the shipwrecks of St Kitts and Nevis, for historical documentation only. One positive result of the terrible tragedy was that many improvements were made and safety standards introduced for ferry transportation between the islands.

The 66 ft steel ferryboat was launched in May 1959, having been built for the government of St Kitts, Nevis and Anguilla (before Anguilla became independent) in Georgetown, Guyana, by Sprostons Limited. The tragic day of the sinking was on a bank holiday weekend. It was customary for many people to travel back and forth between St Kitts and Nevis, some to sell their vegetables and produce, others to visit relatives. Some Nevisians were returning home after a week of work in St Kitts. There were more than 300 men, women and children onboard the MV *Christina*; she had been designed to carry 100 second class passengers, 30 first class passengers and five crew.

It was noted in the official report on the accident that the makers had increased the capacity on the lower deck to 120. This meant the vessel was carrying over double her capacity. Although the sea was calm and the wind light, the overcrowded situation accounted for the accident.

At 3.30 p.m. on that Saturday afternoon the MV *Christina* cast off to begin her final and fatal voyage. It was to be a short voyage of only about half an hour, although she did return to the dock after departure as three latecomers arrived, adding to the crowded conditions. There was hardly any sitting room and passengers were even sitting on handrails and other places where they were not normally allowed. The vessel rolled and rocked unsteadily. The captain was obviously concerned with the trim, as he had his crew rearrange crates of soft drinks. She had a shallow draft of only 4 ft, which allowed her to come alongside the piers, and her double deck had a superstructure of over 13 ft. This construction meant that she was susceptible to rolling, especially on this fateful day when she was very overcrowded on the upper decks and did not have a great deal of cargo to counterbalance the extra weight. One account given for the cause of the accident was that the *Christina* flooded when there was a sudden shift of passengers seeking shelter from an unexpected rain squall. There were also insufficient lifejackets aboard, although it was felt that the boat went down so quickly that there was no time for the passengers to get lifejackets. While a number of passengers got out, and some were rescued by a few small boats which happened to be nearby, many were caught inside and could not escape as the MV *Christina* sank in 11 fathoms of water. There were only 63 survivors. She rests today nearly a mile off Nags Head on the south coast of St Kitts.

The 90 ft MV **Phyllia** was an Antiguan owned cargo ship, the dream of Lionel Thompson, who purchased her in the USA around 1988. She was built in the USA and was approximately 20 years old when he brought her to the islands. Along with a US captain, he sailed her from the United States to Antigua. She was originally named *Big John* and was a 60 berth passenger boat used for deep sea fishing and cruising. Thompson and his brother renamed her and converted her to a cargo vessel. For five years she plied the waters between Puerto Rico, Tortola, St Martin and Antigua, carrying cars and general cargo. She was powered by two 350 h.p. caterpillar engines and was very efficient and fast. In 1993 the MV *Phyllia* was returning to her home base of Antigua from the US Virgin Islands. She stopped to drop cargo in St Kitts. While moored off the harbour she dragged anchor and did damage to a catamaran. The St Kitts port authority impounded her because of the accident. There were legal and financial problems and a dispute about the amount claimed by the owner of the damaged vessel. In the end her owner, not being allowed to move her from the territorial waters of St Kitts and not able to produce the $21,000 US demanded, had to abandon his vessel. She lay at anchor for some time off Basseterre and was eventually washed ashore after a storm. She remained on shore until the St Kitts government decided to sink her. Until research for this book was done, her name was not known and she was locally labelled the *Goat Boat*. She was called this because during the time she was aground, an animal skull became lodged in her wooden decking on the port side near the stern, and coral grew around the area. Even when she was towed to sea the skull remained. Since her sinking, according to St Kitts Scuba, she has been dived on by a visiting veterinary surgeon who has confirmed that the skull, still lodged into the side of the boat, is in fact that of a dog and not a goat.

Enquiries about the boat led me to Al Barker, the agent for this boat during the time she was subject to litigation. After searching old records, Mr Barker found a telephone contact for the owner, a Mr L. Thompson in Antigua. Some years after the sinking, I located the owner. Fortunately he still resides in the same location and was willing to discuss the history and background of the boat. I discovered that the *Goat Boat* was actually the MV *Phyllia*; the name was arrived at by combining Mr Thompson's daughter's name, Lonnica and that of his niece, Phylla. Although she had a sad ending in St Kitts, the *Phyllia* now rests in 80–95 ft of water, on top of a reef, for divers to enjoy.

St Kitts and Nevis are still pristine and relatively unknown in the diving world, so you are unlikely to encounter large groups of divers both under and above the water. There are many unspoiled diving sites and since there has been little shipwreck exploration, you may just chance upon an unknown antique wreck!

# St Lucia

1. *Angelina*
2. *Waiwanette*
3. *Lesleen M*
4. SS *Volga*
5. Porsche car
6. De Havilland aeroplane
7. Bottle site
8. *San Fernando*
9. *Cacique del Carib*
10. *Henry Holmes*
11. MV *Lady Sorcha*
12. Wireless Reef
13. HMS *Cornwall*

St Lucia is one of the few islands in the Southern Caribbean that have realised the value of sunken shipwrecks in attracting not only marine life, but also scuba divers, who enjoy exploring and photographing these sites. In fact, St Lucia is among the leaders in the islands for conservation and protection of its heritage both underwater and above. The dive shops, along with the Fisheries Division, have joined in various efforts to provide some major diving sites, with the result being the intentional sinking of several ships.

Laws protect all of the shipwrecks of St Lucia, and careless divers are not allowed to remove 'souvenirs'. Some of the wrecks divers can explore in St Lucia waters include the *Volga*, an easy dive in 20 ft of water; the *Waiwanette*, an advanced dive, on the southern point of the island; and the *Lesleen M*, the best-known and most often dived wreck.

There are numerous known ancient wrecks, although the exact location of many of these is not generally known. According to Robert Marx, during a hurricane in 1817 seven large British merchant ships

Castries harbour is now home to luxury cruise ships, but beneath the waters at the harbour entrance lie the remains of the *Volga*, and the unlocated remains of the **HMS** *Cornwall*, which sank in 1780

went down on the leeward side of the island and the locations of several are said to be known by local divers.

The *Angelina* is a 45 ft inter-island freighter that lies just outside Marigot Bay. She sits upright on a sandy bottom in 55–75 ft of water. Marigot Bay is very protected, and was used in early days for shelter (incidentally, it is also known as the location for the filming of *Dr Doolittle* in 1967). Antique bottles can still be found on the sandy bottom.

On the southern point of the island is the wreck of the *Waiwanette*, a 273 ft freighter lying in 90 ft of water. The British Sub Aqua Diving Club sank the wreck in early 1984. She had sat unused in Castries harbour for some time. The Fisheries Division and Mel Modson helped set the wheels in motion to have her stripped and the doors welded closed to prevent possible diving accidents. She was then towed from Castries to Vieux Fort for sinking. This is a dive for more experienced divers, owing to its depth and a strong current.

*Lesleen M*, a 165 ft, 400 ton metal freighter, was sunk in June 1986 by the Fisheries Management Division to encourage fish life. She was owned by the McQuilkins of St Lucia (father Newton and son Aubrey) and carried general cargo such as rice, flour and sugar between the islands and South America. She sits upright with her stern in 68 ft of water, on a sandy bottom, just south of the fishing village of Anse La Raye.

The sandy area is also home to a mass of garden eels, gently swaying in the current. The top deck is only 35 ft down and can be seen from the surface. Soft corals and hydroids cover her hull, and small colourful reef fish have taken up residence, with the odd large snapper visiting! The anchor winch, mast, lengths of chain and many of the portholes are still intact. The propeller was also left intact and is covered with growth. With care, more experienced divers can even enter the engine room and hold.

The wreck is inhabited by a variety of macro invertebrates including arrow crabs, seahorses, banded coral shrimp and octopus, and many fish, including angelfish, jacks, snappers and bigeyes. There can be a current, especially on the surface, so this is not an ideal dive for a novice diver.

Just outside Castries, directly under Vigie Point less than 100 yards from the shore, is the wreck of the SS *Volga*. She was an Indian immigrant ship, carrying some 500 East Indian labourers.

On 10 December 1893 the *Volga* was heading into Castries harbour. This was the era when ships were converting from sail to steam, and while the *Volga* had steamship power, on this fateful day she was under sail. The sea was rough as there was a strong groundswell running from the west and an adverse wind. The course forced the captain to tack when he was heading towards Vigie Point and while doing so the ship was forced upon the rocks by the swell. Every ship in Castries harbour rushed to the aid of the 500 passengers and miraculously, not one life was lost. British officers based at Morne Fortune Fort were dining when the accident happened, and in full dress uniforms, hurried to the rescue in small boats. It was said that afterwards they returned to the mess to finish their dinners!

The *Volga* was a navigational hazard to other ships and within several weeks the harbourmaster instructed the ship's agent to remove her. She was blown apart and as the explosions were set she slipped off the ledge to her present resting place. In the early 1980s careless divers plundered the wreck and stripped much off her. All her brass fittings, port holes, lamps and lights were removed. However, some items were recovered by the British Sub Aqua Diving Club and given to the museum. She is an easy dive, lying on a gentle slope in a northwest to southeast direction. The bow lies in only 20 ft of water while the stern is in 60 ft.

Some divers may have read or heard previously about the Porsche car wreck or the De Havilland aeroplane. Owing to deterioration of the **Porsche** wreckage, this site is no longer considered a worthwhile dive site. This car body was intentionally sunk in 45 ft of water in the middle of Anse Chastenet Bay to attract marine life. Before sinking it belonged to the owner of the Anse Chastenet Resort.

Originally sunk near the *Waiwanette* were three aeroplanes, a De Havilland aeroplane, and two US warplanes from World War II, which crashed head on. The **De Havilland aeroplane** had run off the runway of Vigie airport in the early eighties and had been abandoned. It was on a promotional crusade through the islands for the manufacturers. After about two years the local diving club, the British Sub Aqua Diving Club, acquired it. It took two days to tow the plane down the south coast of the island and sink her. To ensure the plane would not float, the team in charge of the sinking filled it with rocks. When the site was dived one week after sinking, the plane was nowhere to be found. The strong currents in the area run north and it is thought that the plane was pulled towards the shore; however, attempts to locate it have been unsuccessful, although it is felt it is still in the area. Perhaps some day it will reappear!

Shipwrecks generate interest in diving for various artefacts, but interesting objects can also be tossed overboard from passing ships. The entrance to Castries harbour is a good diving site for **antique bottle collecting**, although there is limited reef life here, as the bottom is mostly sand. For the avid bottle collector, finding an antique bottle is equally exciting as diving on a living reef. At Half Moon Battery, near the lighthouse, a silver sword handle and military buttons were found and given to the museum by past president of the British Sub Aqua Diving Club, Brian Larkin.

Legends abound about the Spanish galleon ***San Fernando***, including one that a terrible curse was put on her, possibly by the Carib Indians. She supposedly sank in the waters around St Lucia on 13 March 1597. Her manifest is said to have listed a fortune in precious metals coming from Columbia. Robert Marx has seriously researched this vessel but has not confirmed the sinking.

Historian Robert DeVaux has strong doubts that the *San Fernando* was wrecked in St Lucia waters and has made attempts to find more information. According to DeVaux, Tom Ferguson, a prominent historian in St Lucia, told DeVaux when he was around 14 years of age, that the ship's location had been discovered in the early twentieth century. Japanese divers had been brought to St Lucia to salvage the ship.

The massive wooden carving on the bow of the ship was the head of a slave. Soon after beginning the dive, one diver panicked and was pulled from the water by deckhands. Although much of his story was incoherent, he insisted that the masthead was eating his dive buddy. When an attempt was made to pull the second diver from the water all that was recovered was a severed air hose. Tom Ferguson believed that perhaps the diver had crossed the bowhead figure on the bow; the airhose had indeed been caught in the mouth of the figurine and attempts to bring the diver up resulted in the hose being severed, and the diver disappearing.

Around 1980 a Barbados radio station aired a programme called *Caribbean Contact* that reported further on the *San Fernando*. Citing a source from Australia, it reported that the captain of the *San Fernando* was Captain Esquebal. While in South America he fell in love and married a beautiful Indian princess. Upon the return journey to Spain, his new bride was the only female sailing on the *San Fernando*. She was so worshipped by her husband and her beauty was so magnificent that Captain Esquebal had commissioned a life size gold statue to be made in her likeness. This valuable work was onboard ship at the time of her sinking. There was great unrest among the crew, partly because the captain had his new bride aboard. In order to appease the crew before the long voyage home, Esquebal decided he would leave the fleet of ships to make a side trip to St Lucia where Carib Indian women could be captured for his men. It was this fateful decision that led him to run aground. It is said that the Caribs pilfered the ship, killing everyone but the beautiful Indian woman, who became a goddess among them.

It is also said that in 1824 the San Fernando Gold Salvage Company was launched to salvage the ship. The salvage company was said to have located the gold statue and to have been in the process of lifting it when the salvage barge tipped over, losing many of the crew to sharks in the surrounding water. When the salvage operation returned with a larger barge, and secured the sunken ship with a pulley, the attempts to remove parts of the ship resulted in its displacement; it slipped over a ledge and tumbled into the abyss, along with the gold statue of the beautiful Indian princess, to be lost for ever.

On the east coast, the MV *Cacique del Carib* went ashore near Louvet on 9 April 1955. Several attempts were made to tow the 189 ton vessel away from the rocks but it finally broke into pieces. Some lives were lost, and all the cargo. John Evans was awarded a bronze medal for bravery in the effort to save the ship, as he made three attempts by dinghy to take a line to the vessel.

The cable ship *Henry Holmes* was a 978 ton vessel built in 1903 by Napin and Miller in Scotland. She came to the West Indies to lay cable for Cable and Wireless, and was later sold for scrap to the Cul-de-Sac sugar factory. She was scuttled after being stripped in Cul-de-Sac Bay. Local interests purchased the submerged hull when she was in shallow water and planned to fill it with sand and make an island with a restaurant; this never happened. When Hess Oil dredged the bay they dug under the hull and she dropped into a hole about 80 ft deep, where she now rests.

The MV *Lady Sorcha* was a 158 ft, 344 ton British freighter that foundered two miles off Marigot at 5.30 a.m. on 28 August 1975. She had collided with the MV *Whitshope*, a 3000 ton freighter. She sank at the site of the collision in very deep water, which makes her an unsuitable wreck for divers.

Just off Pigeon Island is an area called **Wireless Reef**, located below the fort on a rocky 90 ft drop-off. Although not a shipwreck, this manmade site is worth mentioning. Obsolete telephones and radio equipment belonging to the Cable and Wireless Company were discarded to form an artificial reef. It is said the area is full of lobsters!

C.S. HENRY HOLMES
BUILT 1903 (W. I. & P.T.C.)          SOLD 1935 TO PETER & CO. ST. LUCIA
GROSS TONS 978

**The cable ship *Henry Holmes*, used to lay cable for telephone communications for Cable and Wireless** *(Cable and Wireless)*

Inside Castries harbour, in only 15 ft of (polluted) water, are the remains of the HMS *Cornwall*, which went down in 1780. She has not been located or salvaged, although the St Lucia Historical Society is very interested in this project.

St Lucia offers a good choice of divable wrecks, and should certainly be on the wreck diver's list of islands worth exploring.

# Turks and Caicos

The Turks and Caicos consist of several islands. The wreck sites mentioned here are located around Providenciales and Grand Turk.

## Providenciales

The waters around the island of Providenciales offer one modern-day divable shipwreck, the *WE*. In times past there was also another site which was dived, the **Southwind**, but she is now very broken up and is rarely mentioned as a wreck dive.

The 185 ft **WE** lies on the north side of Providenciales. She was an inter-island freighter which was abandoned and moved around the island to different locations until reaching her final anchorage in Grace Bay. Washed ashore in a storm, she sat on a sandy beach for three years until she was donated to the Watersports Association of Turks and Caicos. They towed her from the beach and sank her in July 1987 to the west of Sellars Cut in the Blue Hills area. She was intended to be put in shallow water but she slipped down the slope and now lies with her bow in 100 ft and her stern in 180 ft. As most of the site is outside the safe sport diving limits, the dive shops do not encourage this site for diving.

One very interesting wreck site which has been completely excavated and studied is the **Molasses Reef Wreck**, so named because of the location where she sank and the fact that her true identity will never be known. Also of great interest is a display on this ancient ship at the Turks and Caicos National Museum. The display occupies the entire first floor of the museum and includes cannons, wooden hull pieces, tailoring tools, carpentry tools and surgical implements. There is useful data on the wreck on the Turks and Caicos National Museum website at www.tcmuseum.org.

The site is located some 20 miles south of Providenciales and is considered the oldest European shipwreck excavated in the western hemisphere. She sank around 1492 or in the early 1500s and for over 450 years lay on the seabed unlocated. Treasure hunters who discovered her in the mid-1970s realised the site was a very early vessel and assumed it might be the *Nina*. The Turks and Caicos government enacted legislation in 1974 that allowed it to take over the site management. Texas A & M University was brought in to excavate the site between 1981 and 1986, headed by Dr Donald Keith. Before the site could be taken over for excavation, rogue treasure seekers dynamited the site and not only did damage but took a number of artefacts. However, many interesting objects were recovered. The ship was armed with heavy artillery, swords, crossbows and grenades. There were fragments of European pottery dating to the late fifteenth century.

It is thought that the ship was a caravel, a fast ship that faciliated the exploration of the New World during the 350 years when Spain had dominance of the New World. There is limited knowledge of these ships, and the technology that allowed these early travellers to cross the Atlantic is not documented. It will never be known why she was in the waters of the Turks and Caicos or what she was carrying. There were four sets of shackles in closed positions. Does this indicate that someone was imprisoned during the voyage, or were they for unruly crew members? Were they only in storage? There was an absence of personal items, perhaps indicating that the crew survived the wreck and were able to take personal effects with them. No anchors were located with the wreck. Perhaps they were lost while the ship was trying to anchor away from the reef or may have been removed by divers before the serious excavation began. These questions will never be answered. Although this wreck site will probably always remain a mystery, it has been a valuable historical find. Any divers interested in historical shipwrecks should visit the Turks and Caicos Museum to view the valuable artefacts on display.

## Grand Turk and Salt Cay

Off the northwest coast of Grand Turk the SS *Harold* lies in only 30 ft of water. She was an iron hulled steamship that ran aground, and can be seen from the shoreline. Parts of her are scattered further offshore.

There is one known and divable British warship in the Turks and Caicos water – the HMS *Endymion*, which lies in only 30 ft of water in a national historical park approximately a 40 minute boat ride south of the island of Salt Cay. This site was originally salvaged by Mr Dean of Salt Cay in 1792 and over the years private divers have salvaged her. The rumors abound on these operations and what was taken.

**HMS *Endymion*, wrecked off the Turks Islands in 1790, is one of the finest examples of an eighteenth-century shipwreck in the West Indies**
*(Robert Bulgin)*

The wooden hulled ship was built in Limehouse, on the River Thames in London, in 1779. For 11 years she served as a warship in His Majesty's Navy, one of 20 vessels of the 'Roebuck class'. *Endymion* was a two deck, 44 gun fifth-rater. She had a complement of 300 men and weighed 938 tons; she was 140 ft on her gun deck with a beam of 38 ft and a draught of 16 ft.

The warship met her fate on 28 August 1790, as she entered the southern approach to the Turk Island Passage. Her commander, Lieutenant Daniel Woodruff, was unaware that an uncharted reef, which later would bear her name, lay directly in the path of the HMS *Endymion*.

Seven minutes before the vessel struck the reef the commander was informed by the master that she was in 7½ fathoms of water. In fact, at the court martial, which was held onboard HMS *Blonde* in Port Royal harbour, Jamaica, on 6 October 1790, the court ordered that pilot John Young attend. As he was too ill he sent a certificate to the court, in which he declared:

*John Young professes himself a pilot for Turk Island Passage, and for the anchorage of the island and the shoals all round the island and the Cays. He believes he has gone through the passage fifty times and declares he never, till the Endymion struck on the rock, or shoal, heard of it and now believes it was not known before that time (signed) John Young, Port Royal Hospital, Jamaica, 6 October, 1790.*

After running aground, Commander Woodruff and his crew remained with the vessel until 6 p.m. on 30 August, some three days. The captain hauled down the colours and quit the ship. There was no loss of life and all were taken safely to Grand Turk aboard the schooners *New Hope* and *Twins*.

There is an extensive account given in the ship's log of the events leading to and after the fateful sinking. Part of this account, as well as interesting line drawings of the ship and of the wreck site, are available on an attractive chart (for details, see below).

She rests in a spur and grove reef system, which provides some protection for the site. She is very encrusted with coral growth but divers can view her 18-pounder guns. Also on the site are iron ballast, lead hull sheathing, tacks, bronze pins, musket and pistol shot, cannon balls and four large anchors. Eighteen of the original 44 cannon remain.

Sometimes described as more of a reef than a wreck site, the actual site does not resemble a ship, having been on the seabed for over 200 years, but the interesting and photogenic artefacts make the site an enthralling and interesting dive.

To order charts with details of the HMS *Endymion* contact:
Wavey Line Publishing
PO Box 101
Grand Turk
Turks and Caicos
BWI

*fax* 649 946 1059   *telephone* 649 941 6009

**Drawing from
a chart of the wreck
of the *Endymion***
*(Wavey Line Publishing)*

# The US Virgin Islands

**St Croix:**
1. *Truck Lagoon*
2. *Northwind*
3. *Suffolk Maid*
4. *Virgin Islander Barge*
5. *Underwater Habitat*
6. *Frederiksted Pier*
7. *Armageddon Plain*
8. *Sondra*
9. Hattaris engine
10. *Rosaomira*
11. *Coakley Bay*
12. *Chez Barge*
13. *Dump Truck*
14. Cessna aeroplane


**St Thomas and St John:**
15. *Cartanser Senior*
16. *Wye*
17. *Rockefeller Wreck*
18. Navy pontoons
19. World War II relics
20. *General Rogers*
21. *Miss Opportunity*
22. WIT *Shoal*
23. SS *Grainton*
24. HMS *Santa Monica*

## St Croix

St Croix ranks highly among the islands of the Eastern Caribbean for known, divable shipwrecks. There are at least 12 wreck sites for divers to explore and photograph, and there are also ancient wreck sites. Off the north of Buck Island there are thought to be the remains of two slave ships. South of the airport, there are bronze cannons in shallow water, indicating an ancient wreck. On the Northstar dive site, a wall dive, two Danish anchors are embedded in the wall, covered with hundreds of years of marine growth suggesting an ancient shipwreck.

The known divable shipwrecks of St Croix are located around the two main towns of the island. Two wrecks are off the capital, Christiansted; the remainder are off Frederiksted.

Butler Bay, off Frederiksted, is home to six shipwrecks and the remains of an underwater habitat. Located near the shipwrecks, in what is called **Truck Lagoon**, there are the remains of around 25 old truck chassis which were put down by Hess Oil to create an artificial reef.

The wrecks of the *Northwind*, the *Virgin Islander Barge* and the *Suffolk Maid*, along with an abandoned underwater habitat, lie within 75 yards of each other, making a unique wreck diving site. The sites can be undertaken as one dive if one is ambitious and swims at a brisk rate. However, they are usually visited on two separate dives, allowing divers to explore the sites in more leisurely fashion.

Nearby lie the *Rosaomira*, the deepest of the wrecks, and the *Coakley Bay*, the newest wreck. In between these sites lies the *Sondra*, a shallow site that can even be snorkelled, although there is not a great deal remaining. Just behind the *Sondra* is the wreck of a small sailing boat.

Although not a wreck site, the famous Frederiksted pier is worth mentioning as an artificial dive site, as is a dive site now called Armageddon Plain, an extension of the pier dive created from the original pilings and material used in the old pier.

There are also two unnamed and little known wrecks off Frederiksted pier. To the north in about 70 ft of water lie the remains of a barge. Before the pier was built, everything was transported to the island on barges and it is thought that this vessel was used for that purpose. It seems a US Navy ship snagged her anchor in the barge, so she is rather broken up. On the south side in 100 ft lie the remains of what is thought to have been a boat that brought lumber to the island.

The **Northwind** is a 75 ft steel hulled ocean tug. She sits upright in 50 ft of water, the closest of a group of three wrecks (*Northwind, Virgin*

The wreck of the
*Northwind*

*Islander Barge, Suffolk Maid*) to the shoreline. She is approximately 300 yards from the shore and a seven minute boat ride from the pier. The shoreline is a jagged, rocky area, however, so does not make a good beach entry. Her top deck is actually only 25 ft below the surface and a permanent mooring makes location by the dive shops easy. Her close proximity to the shore sometimes limits the visibility to around 80 ft.

The *Northwind* was used in the filming of the Hollywood film *Dreams of Gold*, starring Loretta Swit and Cliff Robertson. This was the true story of treasure hunter Mel Fisher's 16-year quest for the Spanish shipwreck the *Atocha*. He finally located the *Atocha* on 20 July 1985, off the Florida Keys, where she sat laden with gold and jewels valued at over $400 million. This was one of history's greatest marine archaeological discoveries. Today Fisher has a museum in Key West, Florida, displaying many of the finds. Filming took place in St Croix during the winter of 1986. The main road of Frederiksted, Strand Street, was used as the town of Key West. Scubawest, the only dive shop in Frederiksted, was used as a local bar in the Key West scenes. The *Northwind* was left behind when the film was completed, tied up alongside the Frederiksted pier. One night in a storm she was banging against the pier, and the US coast guard became concerned that she would do damage to other vessels or become a navigational hazard. The *Northwind* had been turned over to Uwe Ballow, a resident of St Croix at the time, and the coast guard asked him to dispose of her. Commercial diver Tom Long assisted in locating a site in Butler Bay to sink her. Two anchors were put down to hold her in place. She was filled with water and sank to the seabed in May 1986.

**The *Suffolk Maid*, washed ashore by Hurricane Klaus**

The wreck sits on a sandy bottom and is home for a large colony of garden eels. As divers descend they are welcomed by the wonderful sight of the delicate garden eels protruding from their holes on the sandy bottom. They sway back and forth with the gentle current like exquisite ballerinas, feeding on plankton in the water. Stingrays are also often seen, partially covered on the sandy bottom surrounding the *Northwind*. Large French and grey angelfish are seen on nearly every dive.

The **Suffolk Maid** lies about 150 ft to the north. This 144 ft steel hulled ship was a North Sea fishing trawler, brought to the Caribbean in 1981 to be used as an inter-island freighter. However, owing to difficulties, she sat at anchor off Frederiksted from 1981 until 1984.

**Diver Ken Shull on the *Suffolk Maid***

In November 1984 Hurricane Klaus unexpectedly appeared in the islands. As mentioned in the Anguilla chapter, it was the US presidential election day and the US weather satellite was not functioning. Because of the flurry of activities around the election, it seems the satellite was not repaired. The islands were unaware that a hurricane was threating them, and the *Suffolk Maid* was a victim of this unexpected storm. She was washed ashore on top of the pier in Frederiksted, where she sat for over a year. Several unsuccessful attempts were made to pull her off.

The US Navy vessel *Apache* tried to dislodge her and in the attempt, the *Apache* ran aground. She also caused several smaller vessels tied up to the pier to snap their lines. Finally, a salvage company from Puerto Rico was contracted to remove her. The wheelhouse and part of her top structure had to be cut off to lighten the weight, and her engines were removed. This section of the *Suffolk Maid* was dumped in 155 ft of water off the port bow of the *Rosaomira*. After much effort the *Suffolk Maid* was pulled off the pier, but in the strong winds and rough seas the towline snapped. Once again the *Suffolk Maid* was washed ashore, at Monks Bath. Not too many vessels have the misfortune of ending up aground twice in their lives!

After several weeks she was finally escorted to her last resting place 1 mile north of the Frederiksted pier in April 1986.

She sits upright on a sandy bottom in 68 ft of water with her bow in 75 ft. During the years when the *Suffolk Maid* was part of the lives of the people of this community, affection grew for her and a poem, by an unknown author, was written. The dive shop Scubawest provided a copy of this poem, which is a fitting tribute to this lady who now lies on the bottom of the sea.

*Past Present and Future*
*There once was a ship, a rusty little ship,*
*But a ship that floated was she.*
*She went nowhere, she just sat there,*
*Floatin' on the Caribbean Sea.*
*Now she had a name, this ship of fame,*
*She was called the Suffolk Maid.*

*Some diver bold, though she was quite old,*
*Thought she'd make a grand place for fish to stay.*
*There was talk at Whim, 'bout takin' her in*
*And makin' her a man-made reef at Butler Bay.*

*But, one stormy night, she got a fright*
*And on the beach was laid.*
*Her disgrace was spoke by the very folk*
*Who had always ignored Suffolk Maid.*

'Look at that old rusty scow.
No one wants to claim her now'.
So she sat filling with sand and gravel.
'We must rebuild the pier.
That ship can't stay here.
How in the world can we get her to travel?'

The Suffolk Maid sat on land,
Her hull filled with sand and she became a hulk.
So they stripped her down,
Right there in front of the town,
In order to lessen her bulk.

Then one bright day she began to sway
And the tugs pulled her off in one fell stroke.
But the waves were long and the wind was strong
And Suffolk Maid's tow cable broke.

There once was a ship, a rusty little ship,
And again on the beach she was laid.
They all jeered and laughed at this rusty little craft,
The now infamous Suffolk Maid.

But one diver bold, like a very Knight of Old,
Did not desert her.
He stayed on her side
and quietly tried to get her to the Bay of Butler.

It didn't happen fast, but one day at last,
The Maid again floated free.
At the tug's side, she took one last ride,
Floatin' once more on the Caribbean Sea.

With a small sigh, perhaps a goodbye,
She sank that very same day.
For her diver knight she'll always be there;
The Suffolk Maid's at last in Butler Bay.

(Author unknown)

The ***Virgin Islander Barge*** is a massive 300 ft barge that lies only 30 yards from the *Suffolk Maid*. She was originally used as a fuel barge for the Hess Oil Company and was donated for sinking as an artificial reef during 1992. Her stern lies in 60 ft of water and her bow rests in 80 ft.

There is a massive chain lying on her decks. The only openings at the time of writing to view the underside of the barge are small slits, 12 in by 4 ft. Discussions have been held on opening her up for more access. At present, divers can gaze through the slits to the structure underneath; and only small reef fish can enter.

**Diver Ken Shull with a massive chain on the deck of the *Virgin Islander Barge***

The *Underwater Habitat*, an unusual and interesting wreck dive, was a NOAA project, in conjunction with Fairleigh Dickinson University in New Jersey. In discussions held with the director of the project at the time, Mr Richard Berey, an interesting history of the habitat was determined. The habitat, an underwater hydro-lab, was originally used in the late 1960s by the US Navy. She made only two deepwater dives off Hawaii to 600 ft with Navy divers. They were testing equipment and underwater tools to be used by the Navy and also observing the physiological effects on divers. For her use in Hawaii, she was placed on top of a 100 ft steel hulled catamaran and was towed

offshore. She was launched from this for the research projects. For a number of years the habitat then sat on the Molokai pier in Hawaii. In fact, in a number of series of the Hollywood programme, *Magnum PI*, the yellow habitat is seen in the background of some scenes. At that time it was known as the *Agier Habitat*. Jim Miller and Ian Koulich co-authored a comprehensive book on all habitats built worldwide which mentions the *Agier Habitat*.

**The *Underwater Habitat***

Around 1985 or 1986 an old habitat located in Salt River, St Croix, had reached the end of its usable life and was ready to be retired. It was thought that the *Agier Habitat* could be the replacement. The US Navy transported her from Hawaii to St Croix. She sat at the container port for some time. When tests were done it was discovered that the refurbishment would be so expensive it was not feasible, and so she was scrapped.

The habitat was sunk in Butler Bay as a diving site. She lies in 50 ft and has two large 4 ft circular openings on either side, leading to the large inner room where scientists once lived and studied underwater. Divers can easily swim through the entire structure. This is also an interesting photographic site, and home to several large French angelfish.

The manmade dive site at **Frederiksted Pier** is a photographer's dream, especially for invertebrate life. It has been written up over the years in many dive publications. In one account published in *Skin Diver* magazine, well known underwater photographer Stephen Frink commented that a trip to the pier should be mandatory for every diver on the island! He considered it to offer some of the best macro photographs anywhere. Frink was referring to the original pier, which was built around 1965. This had been damaged by Hurricane Hugo in 1989. Also, with the demand for larger cruise ships to come to the island, a deepwater pier was needed. The decision was made to replace the pier and full construction was under way by mid-1993. Initially there was an outcry by the dive operations, concerned that there would be damage to the amazing marine life that had attached itself to the pier. The piles had attracted a mass of multicoloured sponges and all types of invertebrate life. Small marine life such as seahorses, arrow crabs, batfish, and an array of sponges were just a few. In his article Frink commented that the marine life on the pilings was a total ecosystem that had developed over decades and expressed his concern that removal of the pier would cause the loss of this 'unique and world class dive attraction'. Fortunately, many of these creatures are today again to be found on the replacement pier.

Lying to the south of the two main wreck sites of this area are the remains of the original Frederiksted pier, now named **Armageddon Plain**. The site is 90–110 ft deep, and there are some pieces of structure in 140 ft. It consists of large pieces of culverts and pipes, parts of the original pier, scattered across the seabed. There are also pieces of the concrete piling from the new pier, which were sunk at the site. Some of these pieces are over 6 ft across and 30 ft long. A diver can easily swim through them. One lies on a slope and as the diver swims through, exhaled air bubbles slowly roll along the inside of the pipe, exploding in a burst of bubbles at the upper end. The dive shop Scubawest describes the site as 'a swim through a sunken post-apocalyptic city'!

The **Sondra** is 112 ft long, 20 ft wide and lies in 25–30 ft of water on the north side of Fredericksted pier. She is about 300 yards offshore, lying among a patch reef between two bars on Strand Street, Changes in Latitude and the Country Club. There is not much left of the boat, but the engines, the shafts, the prop and a few other parts are still visible. Originally called the *Fort Pit*, she was a submarine chaser during World War II. She was built in Port Calling Boat Works in Midland, Ontario; her keel was laid in 1943 for the Canadian Navy and she was commissioned in 1945. She was one of the last of her kind in service.

While on her very first patrol in the St Lawrence Seaway she was hit by a Japanese torpedo. A 20 ft section was blown out of her and she was disabled. When reconstruction was complete, the war was over.

She was then used as a fisheries patrol boat in Nova Scotia until the Slater brothers purchased her. One of the brothers renamed her the *Sondra*, after his wife. The Slaters were known to purchase war relics with the hope of a profitable sale later. The *Sondra* sat at anchor in Mahone Bay, Nova Scotia, for nearly 20 years. The city port authorities became concerned that the vessel would sink and become a navigation hazard and insisted she be moved. Dave Keller found her in 1974 in Mahone, and purchased her for $1. He spent a year rebuilding her in Nova Scotia.

At that time she had all the original military lockers, which Dave removed. She also had two Vivian 600 h.p. engines (some 38 tons of engine), which are still visible on the seabed where she lies. After her refit Dave moved her to Key West, Florida, living on her for four years before heading south to the islands. For five years the *Sondra* was a floating home as Dave travelled all through the Caribbean islands. Around 1980 he settled in St Croix, still living on the *Sondra*.

In September 1989 Hurricane Hugo roared through the region and as she raged around St Croix, she literally picked up the *Sondra* and grounded her. Dave commented: 'Hugo broke her back; the keel was broken, the ribs were broken.' She was pulled off and anchored, and partially repaired. However, there were numerous leaks and her pumps could not keep up with them. Finally on 10 June 1996 she sank at anchor. Dave, who was on the shore at the time, saw her beginning to sink and was able to rush out and save his two dogs, who were living onboard.

Not far behind the *Sondra*, towards the shoreline, are the remains of a 41 ft **Hattaris** that belonged to Oscar Dravenieks. It seems her generator was removed but the hole was not plugged; she sank at anchor in 1995. Although there is not a lot left on this site, her two 833 h.p. engines remain.

The **Rosaomira**, also called the *Rosa*, is the deepest and among the largest and most impressive wreck dives in St Croix. This 177 ft steel hulled freighter sits upright and the depth ranges from 65 ft on the deck to 110 ft of water under her bow. She was a Venezuelan vessel and arrived in St Croix with cargo. She mistook the Frederiksted pier as her docking location. However, she was then sent to the correct location of the container port, moving in the early hours of the evening. Her captain was pumping ballast from one section of the vessel to make it easier to remove the cargo (pallets of concrete blocks), when, during the night, she accidentally capsized. She was literally floating upside down. Sadly, two of her crew were killed when they were trapped inside. It was discovered that the owner was trying to smuggle diesel fuel, and when the ballast was being transferred the fuel upset the balance of the ship.

The propeller of the
*Rosaomira*

Commercial diver Tom Long, then a St Croix resident, was hired to contain the pollution from the diesel spill and to keep the *Rosa* afloat. For some three weeks he pumped air into her to achieve this. He was also the official interpreter as the captain and the crew spoke only Spanish. A tugboat company from Louisiana was hired to right her, but they were unable to do so. Eventually, Long was hired to move her to Butler Bay and sink her. She was towed to the site by the same tugboat that had tried to right her. This tug would eventually sink, herself, and now lies in 12 000 ft of water off St Croix. The *Rosa* was towed to her final resting place in April 1986. En route, Long climbed on her upside down hull around 12 noon and placed some 16 Tovex explosives on the hull at strategic locations to allow water to enter on one side, with the hope of righting her. At 8 p.m. the first explosives went off. The *Rosa* righted herself and within 15 minutes, sank stern

**The Coakley Bay**

first. Tom Long was the first diver to explore her in the early hours the following day!

The *Rosa's* 6 ft prop is covered in colourful red sponges and encrusting growth, making a splendid photographic site. She originally had two props but careless divers removed one prop, along with portholes, so these are no longer on the site. The superstructure of the vessel is also covered with red and pink encrusting sponges. The hull has attracted a variety of fish. Large black coral trees grow under the bow in 65 ft, making an impressive picture against the white sandy bottom. Evidence of the crew's personal effects, left in the cabins, can be seen. Penetration of the wreck is possible but owing to the depth and the time limit for a safe, no-decompression dive, the dive shops do not encourage this, unless the diver is certified for wreck diving. The site usually has a permanent mooring line attached, so a safety decompression stop is easy to do. From time to time the moorings are cut by propellers and may not always be on the site.

The 89 ft **Coakley Bay** is the newest wreck of St Croix. Built by Levingston in 1951 with a 24 ft beam, for a number of years she served as a harbour tug for the Hess Oil Company; she was repowered in 1980. Her hull number was 470 and her builder's number was 510 1936.

**Sponge growth on the Rosaomira**

She had lived out her time as a tug: she was old, she was rusty, and she had served her usefulness. A decision was made to put her out of commission. The Department of Planning and Natural Resources of St Croix requested she be donated to be sunk as a wreck diving site. After nearly two years of paperwork and obtaining the necessary permits, she was sunk on 15 April 1999 just east of the site of the *Rosaomira*. Hess Oil sank her using their own tugs. Two large Danforth anchors were set (and still remain on the site) and she was then filled with water by two tugs with water cannons. This caused her to sink to the bottom of the seabed.

Her bow originally lay in 56 ft while the top deck was in only 28 ft, making her an ideal beginner's dive. However, during the 1999 hurricane season she was moved into 77 ft of water with her stern in 65 ft. She is now only about 70 ft away from the *Rosaomira*. She was left completely intact when sunk, with her 8 ft prop still in place. In addition there is a control panel on the stern, still working. It controls the rudder, throttle and forward and backward gears. The tug could be manoeuvred from this station. As the site is so new there is only limited

The wheelhouse
of the *Rosaomira*

The control panel
of the *Coakley Bay*

life on her, but she is attracting marine growth. Already there are resident 18–24 in octopuses on the site and many furry sea cucumbers.

There are two wrecks off Christiansted, although only one is regularly dived. *Chez Barge* is the remains of a sand barge, sunk around 1980 by a dive club. Until research was done for this book she had been documented in past writings as having an unknown history and an unknown name. This 110 ft barge is 40 ft wide. She lies upside down in 62–100 ft of water just outside Christiansted.

This is the site of daily fish feeding, developed as a speciality by one of the dive shops, Dive Experience. In fact, they invite divers to 'experience the other end of the food chain – Dining at *Chez Barge*'! The dive is done at 2 p.m. daily because according to Michelle Pugh, owner of Dive Experience, 'if you go earlier, not too many fish are there. I think they have wrist watches'. The site attracts a great variety of fish including parrotfish, yellowtail snappers, black durgeon, Nassau groupers and even jewfish. There are also moray eels in residence. In fact, there are at least seven named residents, including Earl the eel, Wanda the French angelfish, Bruce the queen trigger fish, Sparkly the spotted moray eel, Grover a Nassau grouper, Renegade, a 'fast' green moray and Barbara the Barracuda (named after Barbara Walters)! There are also the remains of a crane protruding from one side of the wreck.

The ***Dump Truck*** site is in 130 ft of water just outside Christiansted harbour east of Scotch Banks. The site is not far from *Chez Barge*. The truck rests on its side on the first drop-off after the bank. Two massive wheels are the first things divers see. There are different stories about how the truck came to be at the bottom of the sea. Some say it fell off a barge in the 1950s, and others that this area used to be a dumping ground. Having been on the seabed for some 40 years there is much growth on the truck and it is also now covered with a few large black coral trees and big sponges. The truck lies on a sandy white bottom, so is an interesting site for underwater photographers. The dive shops do not normally dive this site because there is nothing else nearby and the depth limits the safe time divers have at the bottom. Visibility can be poor because of the location.

There has been mention in past writings on the wrecks of St Croix of the smallest wreck off the island, a two-seater **Cessna aeroplane** that went down in 1978. The pilot ran out of fuel and crashed in only 22 ft of water; he was killed in the accident. The site was divable for some time, but today nothing remains.

## St Thomas and St John

Robert Marx has documented as many as 134 ancient shipwrecks between 1523 and 1833 in his writings on this region. Of course most have not been located, as is the case with many of the old shipwrecks. The divable wrecks are more modern.

The wrecks of St Thomas and St John include the *Cartanser Senior*, the *General Rogers*, the SS *Grainton*, The WIT *Shoal*, the Navy pontoons, the *Santa Monica*, the *Wye*, and *Miss Opportunity*. There is even the wreck of Nelson Rockefeller's private yacht in these waters. All of these wrecks are not easily located and are therefore not dived regularly by the dive shops.

The story of the wreck of the ***Cartanser Senior*** is one of the most dramatic told about an intentionally sunk wreck. The 190 ft Latin American cargo vessel was formerly a World War II freighter. She had been abandoned by her crew in the murky Gregorie Channel when it was suspected that she was being used to transport illegal cargo. She was saved 'in the nick of time' from becoming scrapped on the very day she was scheduled to be destroyed; it was a close call. On 21 March 1979 a blockade of local divers formed a human chain around her to stop her destruction. The company contracted to scrap her, the Ocean Salvers

**Martha Watkins Gilkes holding keel bolts from an ancient wreck**

**'HMS *Pearl* and the *Santa Monica* 14 September 1779' by Thomas Whitcombe** *(National Maritime Museum, Greenwich)*

Inc., decided to postpone the operation rather than attempt to break the chain.

The group of concerned divers had been formed as awareness grew of the fact that the ship had been classified among the derelict vessels in the St Thomas channels. She was scheduled to be cut up and removed by the Corps of Engineers. Although she was derelict, she was completely intact and had all the makings of a great shipwreck for divers. Local commercial diver Pat Boatwright was the first to realise this. As early as 1974 a suitable ship to be sunk as a St Thomas wreck had been sought. At that time location managers for the Hollywood film *The Deep* had checked on a site in St Thomas. As there was not a suitable wreck in St Thomas, the *Rhone* in the British Virgin Islands was selected (see my chapter on the BVIs). Mr Win deLugo, director of the VI Film Promotion Office, was concerned at the lack of a suitable site and at the consequent loss of revenue. Boatwright approached deLugo, who saw the potential of this vessel and contacted the necessary government officials in November 1977. Saving the *Cartanser Senior* was not an easy job, once she had been doomed to destruction.

A diver explores an
ancient anchor

Bureacratic complications made removing her from the list of vessels to be destroyed by the army Corps of Engineers seem impossible. The Corps also advised that there was not time to obtain the needed permits to sink a ship.

Fate intervened and in early 1978 there was a contractor's delay in implementing the destruction of the shipwreck. A 'Save the *Cartanser Senior*' campaign began and grew in the community. The St Thomas Underwater Sports Club became involved, along with Mark Marin and Wydell Robbie. They circulated a petition to 750 people with the aim of creating a marine park with the mighty ship as the focus. This was presented to the governor, Juan Luis, in November 1978. Other groups who joined in the effort included the St Thomas and St John Chamber of Commerce, the Island Resources Foundation, the St Thomas Hotel Association and the St Thomas Historical Trust Inc. Two conservation and cultural affairs officials joined the effort: Robert Mathes, Director of Planning and Development and Paul Adams, Director of Territorial Parks, began work in their departments to make this dream happen. Others who became involved were Dick Doumeng, Senator Alli Paul and Bill Evans. In the final effort these three were among the five private citizens who, together with the dive shops, put up money to pay for the sinking.

The US *Skin Diver* magazine joined in the effort and editor Paul Tzimoulis devoted editorials to the project. He also made the comment: 'Once it goes in the water the shipwreck becomes an important natural resource. It is worth millions of dollars for the tourist economy.'

On 22 March, the day after the human blockade had stopped her immediate destruction, the Lt. Governor of St Thomas, Henry Millin, was contacted by the Corps of Engineers, confirming that the *Cartanser Senior* would be deleted from the contract. The wreck became the responsibility of the Virgin Islands government.

It seemed that she was saved and the divers who had fought so hard to prevent her from being cut to pieces breathed a sigh of relief; however, that was not the end of the story. For two years the campaign continued for the raising and relocation of the ship. The estimated costs were staggering: over $200,000 US. It seemed impossible that this could be raised.

During this time another misfortune occurred in St Thomas waters, for the cruise ship *Angelina Lauro*; her tragedy would eventually be the salvation of the *Cartanser Senior*. The *Angelina Lauro* was on a visit to St Thomas when she caught fire on 30 March at the West Indian Company dock. She burned for five days, was gutted by the flames and sank on site. Eventually a salvage contract was awarded to Neptune Transport and Services of Sweden. This worldwide leading salvage company was responsible for refloating the cruise ship and the job required an 800 lb crane. This sort of work is very expensive – around $25,000 US per day. It was estimated it would take at least ten days and the crane would have to come from headquarters in Southampton, England. This quote was in line with the others given to raise and relocate the *Cartanser Senior*. Suddenly it became evident to those involved in the effort that this crane, coming to St Thomas to refloat the *Angelina Lauro*, could help in the raising and relocation of the *Cartanser Senior*. The president of the company in Sweden was contacted. It was agreed that for a nominal fee of $30,000 the crane could be utilised for this additional job.

On 16 July 1979, with the help of the giant crane, the *Cartanser Senior* was raised from the waters of Back Bay and towed just off Capella (Buck Island). There was concern that the lifting might break the ship, but she was successfully relocated intact. The day after she was sunk, more than 150 people were diving and snorkelling on this 'Champagne dive of the Caribbean' as she was dubbed by Senator Alli Paul.

Remains of old barges off St Thomas

She is now a very popular site for beginners and seasoned wreck divers. She lies on her port side at a 45° angle on a flat bottom with her bow in 35 ft and her stern in 40 ft. She originally had two brass propellers, but these are gone. Since her sinking several storms and hurricanes have damaged her but she is still an exciting dive. Hurricanes David and Frederick moved the wreck; Hurricane Hugo broke her into three pieces. Given her chequered past and the saga of her sinking, this is one site all divers to St Thomas should explore. She is an especially exciting night dive.

Also lying in St Thomas waters, to the southwest off Buck Island, is the Royal Mail Steamer *Wye*. She was a victim of the 1867 hurricane that sank the Royal Mail Steamer *Rhone* in the British Virgin Islands. In an article in *Atlantic and Pacific Breezes* (issue 24, summer 1965), T.A. Bushell talks about the search for the *Wye* by American divers:

*First they circled Buck and Capella Islands. When that failed they climbed the rocks along the whole of the eastern side of Buck Island to see if they could locate the remains of the engines. These, of the steeple type, were reported in 1867 to have remained wedged in the rocks after the hull had disintegrated under the onslaught of the hurricane.*

Today little remains of the scattered ruins.

The 100 ft steel hulled luxury boat of American tycoon Nelson **Rockefeller** lies in 20 ft of water off Flat Key, although there is not a great deal left at the site. During the 1950s she was under way on a dinner cruise when her captain ran her aground. All guests and crew were safely rescued, but the boat did not survive the accident. Needless to say, Rockefeller did not enjoy his dinner that evening!

Inside Triangle Reef the remains of three large **Navy pontoons** are found. These are 50 ft wide and 100 ft long and lie in only 30–35 ft of water. They were flat vessels, with no engines, and were used to carry heavy cargo, under tow. It is thought they sank in the 1940s or 1950s. Before Hurricane Hugo, local divers claimed they were like coral forests, but much of the coral has been damaged.

South of the so-called Porpoise Rocks in 80 ft of water there are a variety of **World War II relics**. This site used to be a dumping ground for the government and is home to not only an assorted collection of wreck parts, but a great deal of marine life.

The ***General Rogers*** is a 120 ft steel hulled auxiliary coast guard vessel that was used as a buoy tender. She was decommissioned and much of her superstructure was removed to prevent her becoming

**The wreck of the General Rogers**

a navigational hazard. The coast guard sank the *General Rogers* in 1972 and sadly, while she was being sunk, one of the crew members drowned. She now lies between St Thomas and Thatch Island in 65 ft of water with the main deck in only 45 ft. She supports a wide variety of marine life and divers enjoy exploring her.

In deeper water (about 100 ft), lies the ***Miss Opportunity***. For some time in the early 1980s she was used as government offices, off Frenchtown. When she became dilapidated, it was decided to sink her to make an underwater reef. She rests on her port side, and divers enter through the stern.

The West Indies Trading ship (WIT) ***Shoal*** is located southwest of the airport, by Crown Bay. She was a 327 ft cargo freighter owned by West Indies Transport. In 1984 she was being moved to a site to be sunk, having lived out her usefulness. She had been temporarily patched for the trip. However, about two miles off Charlotte Amalie, she began taking on water and had to be released. She sank slowly to the bottom. She sits upright with her keel in 75 ft of water, but the wheelhouse is a mere 30 ft from the surface; her main decks are in 70 ft. There is a large broken crane, now coral encrusted, that lies along the ship. Three large cargo holds are open, allowing divers easy entry. The WIT *Shoal* lies on a sandy bottom, covered in marine growth; large schools of fish, such as horse-eye jacks, inhabit her. During Hurricane Marilyn in September 1995 there was structural damage but there is still plenty to explore. The site can have strong currents, so divers need to dive with experienced divemasters who know the site.

The SS ***Grainton***, originally a Great Lakes grain carrier, is known as the *Grain Wreck*. Badly broken up, the wreck is not recognisable. The 450 ft ship lies in 105 ft of water, although parts of her are in 60 ft. She was sunk in the early 1970s and has a profusion of fish life on her. There is still a hugh anchor on the site.

The scanty remains of the HMS ***Santa Monica*** lie in Round Bay, a part of Coral Bay off St John. She sank in 1782. Although she had been dived on for many years by local divers, she was 'officially' discovered in 25 ft of water in the summer of 1970 by John Roy, who worked with the Caribbean Research Institute at the College of the Virgin Islands. In the spring of 1971 the Caribbean Research Institute started excavation work, and this was completed in June 1973.

The *Santa Monica* was a 28 gun frigate belonging to Spain. She was on a routine patrol off France. The HMS *Pearl*, a British Royal Navy ship, captured her and escorted her to the Royal Naval dockyard in Portsmouth, England (see p. 140). She was taken into the British Royal Navy under her own name and for some time worked with the English Channel fleet on patrol. She was sent to the West Indies in 1781 under the command of Captain John Linzee.

The British Virgin Islands government had appealed to the British West Indies commander for protection, as there was the possibility of an attack on Tortola by the French and Americans. Four ships were sent to provide the requested protection. The *Santa Monica* was the flagship in this fleet.

In an account sent to the Admiral of English Harbour, Antigua, Captain Linzee reported that on 1 April 1782, his ship struck an unknown rock 2 miles out to sea from Norman Island in the British Virgin Islands. In the court martial that followed, a local ship's captain who knew the waters well confirmed that the rock was not noted on charts or known to him or other seasoned local sailors. The result of the court martial was acquittal for the officers and crew, as the loss of the ship was deemed to have been an accident. After striking the rock, the ship was taking on so much water that the captain made for the nearest harbour, at Coral Bay, St John, to save lives and stores. In order to save what he could the captain had to put the ship onshore in 3½ fathoms (19 ft).

In fact, when the site was discovered over two centuries later, the main part of the ship was resting in shallow water but the stern protruded over a drop-off to 50 ft. The shallow part of the wreck had already been fully explored by local divers so the excavation was done on the 'relatively untouched mid and stern sections'. The final reports indicated that the most significant finds were the broken and intact ceramics. At this period in history there was great change in the ceramic industry in England and this was evident from the artefacts recovered. At this time, officers and men provided their own dishes. There were a great many fragments of dishes found with the word 'Wardroom' painted on them. Those studying the site concluded that the officers might have used their own funds to buy a set of dishes for the wardroom.

Other interesting artefacts were ornate brass fittings from furniture, and ship's fittings. Because the ship sank in shallow water, many items were recovered at the time including cannon, masts, sails, and personal effects.

This site is now not recognisable as a shipwreck and snorkellers and divers should not expect to see too much. The wooden structure long ago deteriorated, and only the lower sections covered by sand remain.

The US Virgin Islands are particularly rich in wreck sites and the variety on offer, with both ancient sites and those recently sunk, small and large vessels, and depths ranging from 15 ft to over 100 ft, provides something for all divers, whatever their level of experience.

# St Vincent and the Grenadines

Wreck diving is available in St Vincent, as on every island in the Caribbean, but it is not strongly promoted because of the depths of the wrecks. Shallower wreck sites of interest are to be found in the Grenadines. Robert Marx, in *New World Shipwrecks 1492–1825*, lists seven ancient wrecks in the waters off St Vincent. He also records that in 1635 two Spanish merchant ships were wrecked off the southeastern tip of the island and that survivors were found some 32 years later, in 1667, when English settlers arrived on St Vincent.

Known, divable wreck sites are more modern, however. There are three wrecks together in Kingstown harbour. On 21 November 1984 the 120 ft steel hulled freighter **Seimstrand** collided with another freighter, the **Nomad**, and both sank, so that they now lie next to each other. In deeper water the remains of a much more ancient ship were located, which have now become a major archaeological project.

Until November 1999 the top deck of the *Nomad* was in only 15 ft of water, with a gradual slope to 40 ft. Hurricane Lenny cut the wreck in two and she slid down to 70 ft. The *Seimstrand* was just behind the *Nomad* in 60 ft sloping down to 80 ft until Hurricane Lenny moved her to 100 ft. These wrecks had been an ideal wreck dive, as divers could start their dive on the deeper site and end in only 15 ft of water – an ideal decompression stop. Unfortunately, owing to the depths and the limited time available underwater on these sites since the hurricane shifted them, the dive shops no longer promote wreck diving here.

The ancient wreck site in Kingstown harbour is also in 100 ft, and from December 1997 has been the subject of an archaeological investigation conducted by the Institute of Maritime History (IMH). This was a joint project supported by the St Vincent government, the Organization of American States (OAS), the Academic Diving Program at Florida State University and the Nautical Archaeology Program at Texas A & M. The site was originally thought to be the British slave ship *Africa*, which according to Robert Marx (*Shipwrecks in the Americas*, 1987), was lost in Kingstown harbour in

The wreck of the *Seimstrand* in St Vincent harbour

1784. There was much cookware on the site which could have suggested a slave ship, but a warship or privateer with a large crew would have been similarly equipped. There was also speculation that the ship could have been HMS *Cornwall*. Several cannon were located, encrusted in the reef. One cannon was raised and this confirmed that the ship was actually a French warship; the date on the cannon was 1776. The conservation work on the cannon should soon be completed. It will eventually be on display on St Vincent, along with other artefacts.

I had the good fortune to dive on this site in the early 1990s, when little was known about it; Bill Tewes, owner of Dive St Vincent, had dived on the wreck for years but had only taken divers down to see a few exposed artefacts, including a cannon and a large anchor, leaving the site undisturbed. Hurricane Lenny also affected this site, covering up some of the cannon.

Even though the wreck is not actively dived because it is a protected site and because of its depth, for the historically minded diver this is an interesting wreck to read about and research. Divers who may be allowed to dive the site should remember that it has a 'no touch and no recovery policy' and cannot be disturbed. More information can be found at the website http://maritimehistory.org/st_vincent/intro.html, which features the project.

**Bottle Reef**, located in the Kingstown harbour, begins as a gentle slope with small wall starting at 25 ft and dropping to 91 ft. Although this is not a wreck site, it is interesting because of the artefacts located in the area. The wall is adorned with gorgonians, sea fans, sponges and black coral. Solitary Spanish mackerel glide by. During tarpon season (February to June) these sleek, silver giants enhance the site. An added treat is the chance of finding an antique bottle. Fort Charlotte, a British fort built between 1796 and 1806, is perched above the site and it is thought that the bottles scattered about were tossed over from the fort. If there is a strong current the site is limited to advanced divers.

To the south, the Grenadine islands of Union, Canouan, Mayreau, Mustique and Bequia, which belong to St Vincent, also offer some wreck diving opportunities.

The *Gladdie* is a 65 ft wreck lying in 90 ft of water, port side down. She was a cement sailboat and in her sailing days plied the waters around the islands. The *Gladdie* is intact and divers can swim through the superstructure. She was deliberately sunk in 1978 by the Bequia authorities as a diving site. Spadefish, large angelfish and green moray eels are often seen, and the occasional nurse shark. The site is an advanced dive because of its depth.

The **Rick's H** also lies off Bequia, just below Moon Hole. This 150 ft wreck lies in 115 ft of water. It was broken into three pieces by Hurricane Lenny in 1999. The site has many lobsters, turtles and other interesting marine life.

The 110 ft **Lireco** is located off the Isle de Quatre. She was a freighter and was deliberately sunk in 1986 as a diving site. There can be very strong currents in the area and the dive is considered an advanced one. The *Lireco* sits upright and divers can penetrate her engine room, where much equipment still remains.

The wreck of
the cruise ship *Antilles*

Near Mustique the wreck of the **Antilles** lies as a testament to the danger of running aground, for this was once a great cruise ship. The 400 ft vessel hit the reef many years ago during a cruise and was never pulled off. An 80 ft salvage tug also lies near her. The site is very exposed and the currents make for dangerous or even impossible diving conditions. Most of the wreck is broken and flattened but there are still interesting artefacts and structure to see.

The wreck of the **Jonas** is a 65 ft cement boat that was sunk as a diving site at Montezuma's Reef. It sits on top of the coral reef in 40 ft of water. Off Canouan is the MV **Shadow**. For nearly two years she had been at anchor, so already had much growth on her when she sank.

One of the favourite sites dived in this area is the 140 ft World

War I English gunboat HMS **Purina**, which lies just off Mayreau in only 40 ft of water, with the top deck in a mere 23 ft, making this an ideal beginner's dive. The HMS *Purina* was built by A.G. Munford, Colchester. She was a merchant ship commissioned for use by the Royal Navy. On 29 August 1918, during a normal patrol when the British were protecting the area, the HMS *Purina* hit the reef and immediately sank, sitting upright in the shallow water. She is totally intact with boilers, several heads and two massive props still in place. Owing to the shallow depth she is totally encrusted with luxuriant growth of hard and soft corals. Lobsters and octopus are found tucked in many nooks and crannies, along with numerous invertebrate creatures.

St Vincent is becoming known for unusual marine life such as frog fish, seahorse and pipe blennies, and the dive shops promote this aspect of diving rather than wreck sites. However, the dedicated wreck diver can find sites to explore.